A Triduum Sourcebook II

A Triduum Sourcebook

Compiled by
Joan Halmo
Frank Henderson

Art by
Linda Ekstrom

Liturgy Training Publications

Acknowledgments

This book collects materials from numerous sources. We are grateful to these publishers and authors. Every effort has been made to determine the ownership of all texts and to make proper arrangements for their use. We will gladly correct in future editions any oversight or error that is brought to our attention.

Acknowledgments for sources will be found in the endnotes.

Editor: Kathy Luty
Production Editor: Theresa Pincich
Editorial Assistants: Rolando Gonzalez, Lorraine Schmidt
Layout: Jill Smith
Production Artist: Jim Mellody-Pizzato
Series Designer: Michael Tapia

Copyright © 1996, Archdiocese of Chicago, Liturgy Training Publications, 1800 North Hermitage Avenue, Chicago IL 60622-1101; 1-800-933-1800; FAX 1-800-933-7094. All rights reserved.

Printed in the United States of America.

Library of Congress Cataloging-in-Publication Data

A triduum sourcebook / compiled by Joan Halmo and
    Frank Henderson ; art by Linda Ekstrom.
            p.   cm.
    ISBN 1-56854-099-X
        1. Paschal triduum — Liturgy. 2. Catholic Church — Liturgy.
    I. Halmo, Joan, 1945- . II. Henderson, Frank (J. Frank)
    BX2015.785.T75 1996
    264'.02 — dc20   95-48135
                                                          CIP

TRID/R

Contents

O N this holy night, called the "mother of all vigils," the church keeps watch, celebrating the resurrection of Christ in the sacraments and awaiting his return in glory. It is the turning point of the Triduum, the passover of the new covenant which marks Christ's passage from death to life. *Roman Missal*

I F one should inquire about the reasons why we keep such a vigil, the answer is easy to find and give. For he who has granted us the glory of his name has illuminated this night: he to whom we say "Thou shalt enlighten my darkness" enlightens our hearts, so that just as our eyes rejoice at this splendor of lighted candles so our mind may be enlightened and shed light on the meaning of this resplendent night.

Why, then, is it that Christians keep vigil on this anniversary night? For this is our greatest vigil and no other vigil of similar proportions is known. In answer to our eager query, When do we keep vigil? we reply: Several other vigils are kept by us, but nothing comparable to this vigil. The apostle has urged the faithful to frequent fastings and vigils recalling his own practice in the words: in fastings often, in many sleepless nights (2 Corinthians 11:27). But tonight's vigil is so special that it deserves to appropriate to itself the common title of vigil. Augustine
Fifth century

S ISTERS and brothers in Christ,
on this most holy night
when our Savior Jesus Christ passed from death to life,
we gather with the church throughout the world
in vigil and prayer.
This is the passover of Jesus Christ:
Through light and the word,
through water and the bread and wine,
we recall Christ's death and resurrection,
we share Christ's triumph over sin and death,
and with invincible hope *Book of*
we await Christ's coming again. *Common Worship*

D EAR friends in Christ,
on this most holy night,
when our Lord Jesus Christ passed from death to life,
the Church invites its sons and daughters
throughout the world
to come together in vigil and prayer.
This is the passover of the Lord:
if we keep the memory of his death and resurrection
by hearing his word and celebrating his mysteries,
then we may be confident
that we shall share his victory over death
Roman Missal and live with him for ever in God.

O night more light than day,
more bright than the sun,
O night more white than snow,
more brilliant than many torches,
O night of more delight than is paradise.

Night devoid of all dark,
O night dispelling sleep
and teaching us the vigilance of angels,
O night the demons tremble at,
night of all nights in all the year desired.

Night of the church's bridal,
night of new birth in baptism,
night when the devil slept and was stripped,
Asterius of Amasea night when the heir took the heiress
Fourth century to enjoy their inheritance.

DEAREST brothers and sisters, we keep vigil on this night, on which we recall that our Lord was buried. We ought to keep vigil during that time in which, for our sakes, he slept. Long before, he announced his passion through his prophet: "I slept," he says, "and I rose up, because the Lord received me" (Psalm 3:5). He called the Father "Lord." Hence on the night on which he slept, we keep vigil, so that through the death he suffered we might have life. During his short sleep we celebrate a vigil, so that he will keep watch for us and, when we are raised, we can abide untired for the eternal vigil. On this night he also rose; our hope keeps watch for his resurrection.

Augustine
Fifth century

O splendor of eternal light,
    Who in full glory dwell on high!
The world began as light from Light,
All goodness in the Father's sight.

Upon the twilight chaos played
Your wisdom forming night and day.
As night descends to you we sing
To hover near on brooding wing.

Medieval Latin hymn

FOUR nights are written in the Book of Remembrance,
    which lies open before the Lord.
The first: when God was revealed in the creation.
The second: when God was revealed to Abraham.
The third: when God was revealed in Egypt,
        slaying the firstborn of the Egyptians
        and saving the firstborn of Israel.
The fourth: when God will liberate the people of Israel
        from captivity among the nations.

Targum Onkelos

A T midnight the LORD struck down all the firstborn in the land of Egypt, from the firstborn of Pharaoh who sat on his throne to the firstborn of the prisoner who was in the dungeon, and all the firstborn of the livestock. Pharaoh arose in the night, he and all his officials and all the Egyptians; and there was a loud cry in Egypt, for there was not a house without someone dead. Then he summoned Moses and Aaron in the night, and said, "Rise up, go away from my people, both you and the Israelites! Go, worship the LORD, as you said. Take your flocks and your herds, as you said, and be gone. And bring a blessing on me too!"

So the people took their dough before it was leavened, with their kneading bowls wrapped up in their cloaks on their shoulders.

The time that the Israelites had lived in Egypt was four hundred thirty years. At the end of four hundred thirty years, on that very day, all the companies of the LORD went out from the land of Egypt. That was for the LORD a night of vigil, to bring them out of the land of Egypt. That same night is a vigil to be kept for the LORD by all the Israelites throughout their generations.

Exodus 12:29–32, 34, 40–42

T HIS is the night which we celebrate with a vigil because of the coming of our King and God. There are two reasons for the choice of this night: First, after his suffering he rose from the dead on this night; and second, he shall receive the kingdom of the world also on this night.

Lactantius
Fourth century

FROM the beginning of the world's creation until this time, the course of time was so divided that day preceded night, according to the order of its primeval making. On this night, because of the mystery of our Lord's resurrection, the order of time was changed. He rose from the dead during the night, and on the following day he showed the effect of his resurrection to his disciples. Having shared a feast with them, he proved the truth of his power as they wondered and rejoiced. Most properly was night joined to the light of the following day, and the order of time so settled that day would follow night. It was once appropriate that night follow day, for by sinning the human race fell away from the light of paradise into the darkness and hardships of this age. It is appropriate that day follow night now, when through faith in the resurrection we are led back from the darkness of sin and the shadow of death to the light of life by Christ's gift. Wherefore, dearly beloved, we who have come to know that this special night has been illumined by the grace of our Lord's resurrection must also take particular care lest any least part of it become dark in our hearts. All of it should become light as day for us, especially now when we are keeping vigil with the devotion of worthy praise, and are awaiting with a pure and sober conscience the feast of Easter Sunday when we have completed this vigil.

Bede the Venerable
Eighth century

A t midnight came the cry: Here comes the Bridegroom, go out to meet him! Yes, it will be very late at night, when everyone is fast asleep, without a care in the world, that Christ will make his coming heard through the shouts of angels and the trumpets of powers which go before him. Perhaps it will help the reader to know that Jewish tradition tells us that the Messiah will come at midnight, as happened in Egypt, when they celebrated the Pascha, and the Exterminator came, and the Lord passed over the dwellings, and the doorposts of our foreheads were consecrated with the lamb's blood. This is why I think we also have an apostolic tradition that on the day of the paschal vigil the people should not be dismissed before midnight while they await the coming of Christ, and after that time has passed and they

Jerome   presume they are safe (they may be dismissed) with every-
Fifth century   one keeping the festal day.

T HIS is the great night of the *mysterium,* the night that is to give birth to new life. For the unbaptized it brings initiation; for the baptized, renewal; for the penitents, a call back to life already possessed. On all, then, hope presses. No one thinks of sleep. No day is so longed for as this night is; watchful longing runs ahead of the weary hours. Finally the sun goes down. This earthly moment is holy, for it saw the creation of the world which God called into being in springtide. It is also the moment for the new creation of grace, the springtide of the whole world. Dumb things are to speak and speakers will learn to listen. Now all creatures are to speak the language of symbols, and people will understand. It is the hour of mysteries.

Aemiliana Löhr   The faithful know what is happening: God is at work.

THE only place we can begin is in the dark, the dark of a Saturday night and Sunday morning. People are quietly assembling. They may be many or few. They come as individuals, couples, households, friends. Some of them are light-headed from 48 hours of a strict fast; they are hungry to be in this assembly tonight.

Gabe Huck

O Night clearer
than day
Night when love
comes from the tomb
Night that frees
Jesus from the snare
Night more shining
than snow
Night more burning
than flames
O night clearer
than day

O night sweeter
than heaven
Night of wakefulness
for all the Body
Night when the breath
fills the earth
Night that glitters
with light
Night of the victory

that kills death
O night sweeter
than heaven

O night greater
than peace
Night that clouds
the hidden world
Night when grace
shines in glory
Night that draws
our history
Night that pours off
the impure heart
O night greater
than peace

O night stronger
than time
Night of life
after death
Night of speech
for all silence
Night when the church
comes to birth
Night of flowing water
after the frost

Commission
Francophone
Cistercienne

O night stronger
than time

WHEN I was a child, the Easter Vigil was a profound event for me. I didn't know what was going on, but I did know they were doing everything I liked. They were playing with fire. They were playing with water. They were singing things I didn't understand. He was blowing on the water! He was splashing the water on people! The air was full of smoke. It was dark and it was scary. It was everything that I loved.

Tom Shepard

WAKE up, wake up, ye sleepy souls,
And be alive and don't be dead,
There is no time to sleep I say,
Now in this great and glorious day.

Don't be sleeping there so sound,
Get up yourselves and stir around.
For if you want to keep awake,
Arise and give a mighty shake.

Shaker song
Nineteenth century

WHAT keeps us from sleeping
is that
they have threatened us with resurrection.

Accompany us, then,
on this vigil
and you will know
how marvelous it is
to live
threatened with resurrection.

Julia Esquivel

THE paschal mystery, already celebrated in various ways since the Mass of the Lord's Supper, is clearly and joyfully announced from the very beginning of the Vigil liturgy. The service of light, culminating in the great Easter proclamation of the resurrection, establishes from the outset the meaning of the celebration. It is in the light of the Easter candle that the scriptures are read, understood and received. They unfold the wonderful story of God's work of creation and recreation. Then, those chosen for Christian initiation are plunged into the waters of Jesus' death and resurrection and are anointed by the Spirit. The whole assembly of the faithful renew the promises of their baptism, and, finally, gathered at the table of the Lord, all celebrate Christ's triumphant sacrifice and share the sacrament of his body and blood.

In this way, in accord with most ancient tradition, this night is kept as a vigil for the Lord. The gospel of Luke reminds the faithful to have their lamps burning, to be like servants awaiting the return of the head of the household who, on arriving, will find them awake and will seat them at the family table.

Roman Missal

TO those who are not of the household of faith, what we are about to do must look very peculiar. We are about to stand in the dark, carry candles about, sing lengthy and sublime religious texts, read stories from the Bible. What does this all mean? What is going on here in this community?

I think that I first came to understand what this was all about and why I came to think that this was the most important thing in my life when I read *The Lord of the Rings* by J. R. R. Tolkien. In their wandering and meandering, two of the main characters, called hobbits, meet a talking tree, called an Ent, and they introduce themselves and the conversation proceeds:

"I'm a Brandybuck, Meriadoc Brandybuck, though most people call me just Merry."

"And I'm a Took, Peregin Took, but I'm generally called Pippin or even Pip."

"Hm, but you are hasty folk, I see," said Treebeard. "I am honored by your confidence; but you should not be too free all at once. There are Ents and Ents, you know; or there are Ents and things that look like Ents but ain't as you might say. I'll call you Merry and Pippin, if you please — nice names. For I am not going to tell you *my* name, not yet at any rate." A queer half-knowing, half-humorous look came with a green flicker into his eyes. "For one thing it would take a very long while: My name is growing all the time, and I've lived a very long, long time; so my name is like a story. Real names tell you the story of the things they belong to in my language, in the Old Entish as you might say. It is a lovely language, but it takes a very long time to say anything in it, because we do not say anything in it, unless it is worth taking a long time to say, and to listen to."

To use Treebeard's mode of expression, we are not going to be hasty folk tonight satisfied with glibly saying the name "Christian." Tonight, you might say, is "Old Entish" night in the church. Tonight we are going to tell our name — to ourselves, by way of reminder, to those who will become part of us this night through baptism and confirmation, and to those of the world who will listen, who will take the time to hear what our name is.

And our name is a very long one, one that has been growing since the creation of the world. Our name is a very long story — of how we were made, of how God chose us from among all peoples, of how God liberated us from bondage, of how God planted us in the promised land, of how, in these last times, God has given the story a new twist, given our name meaning in the life, death and resurrection of Jesus.

Because we have been here for so long, it takes a long time to tell who we are, to recount the story of our life as a people. And none of us would be here if we did not think that name was worth telling and listening to. Now the trick to this kind of name-telling is to relax. You cannot be hasty in this time ahead of us. Haste will stop up your ears finally, and then you will not hear this lovely language and our beautiful name.

Relax and make yourself comfortable in the darkness and don't even try to "make sense" of the name. Just hear it, let it roll over you in waves of meanings. Tonight we are going to listen to a series of episodes, not write a theological treatise on the resurrection. A practical word about relaxing: if you need to get up and move about, do so. If you need a breath of fresh air, go out to get it. We'll still be telling the story when you rejoin us. Whatever you need to do to stay comfortable, do it. All of this will enable you to hear the lovely language in which we can really name ourselves as God has named us.

"Christian" is merely an inadequate abbreviation for what we are about to tell.

Brian Helge

B LESS the Lord,
all who serve in God's house,
who stand watch
throughout the night.

Lift up your hands
in the holy place
and bless the Lord.

And may God,
the maker of earth and sky,
bless you from Zion.

Psalm 134:1 – 3

A LMIGHTY and eternal God,
you created all things in wonderful beauty and order.
Help us now to perceive
how still more wonderful is the new creation,
by which in the fullness of time
you redeemed your people
through the sacrifice of our Passover, Jesus Christ,
who lives and reigns forever and ever.

*Book of
Common Worship*

FAITHFUL God,
you placed the rainbow in the skies
as the sign of your covenant with all living things.
May we who are saved through water and the Spirit,
worthily offer to you our sacrifice of thanksgiving.

*Book of
Common Worship*

GRACIOUS God of all believers,
through Abraham's obedience
you made known your faithful love
to countless numbers.
By the grace of Christ's sacrifice,
fulfill in your church and in all creation
your promise of a new covenant.

*Book of
Common Worship*

GOD of steadfast love,
your wonderful deeds of old shine forth
even to our own day.
Through the waters of the sea
you once delivered your chosen people from slavery,
a sign for us of the salvation of all nations
through the grace of Baptism.
Grant that all of the peoples of the earth
may be numbered among the offspring of Abraham,
and rejoice in the inheritance of Israel.

*Book of
Common Worship*

Roman Missal

THE people assemble around a bonfire. Its flames dispel the darkness and light up the night. The beauty of the fire, its warmth and its light, draw the liturgical assembly together as the people arrive.

THE vigil begins, as it were, with an act of ritual arson. We light this fire not because spring nights are chilly, not because our pagan ancestors greeted the equinox with bonfires on hillsides, not even because our forebears in faith were led by "a pillar of cloud by day, a pillar of fire by night" — but because *kindling a fire is a daring, dangerous and destructive thing to do.* The world as we know it has to be torched. (Local fire marshals, take note! We're doing this on purpose! Arrest us if you dare!) The fire is to the vigil what the Big Bang was to the universe: an explosion so uncontrollably vast in its magnitude, so awesome in its energy, so fierce in its power to destroy and create, that light and radiation from it are still not spent these billions of years later.

Nathan D. Mitchell

ON the Easter Eve the church functions, and presents itself, as the *watchful one,* who knows that "the night is advanced and the day of Christ is at hand"; as the *waiting one,* who keeps herself in readiness for the coming of the Lord in order to be able to open the door for him when he suddenly stands before it and knocks; and as the *hungry one,* who yearns for the union with her bridegroom at the eternal wedding breakfast. Not knowing when the Lord will come, "whether in the evening, at midnight, at cock-crow, or in the morning," the church remains wakeful, like the servants in the gospel; and like the wise virgins, it waits with lamps burning until the hour comes when the cry is heard: "See, the bridegroom comes! Let us meet him!"

Hansjakob Becker

B E here among us, light in the midst of us.
Be here among us, light in the midst of us.
Show your glory for us to see.
    Stir up your power and come to our rescue.

Be here among us, bring us to life.
    Be here among us, flame of our life.
Flame of our life, God in the midst of us,
    Come to our rescue, bring us to life.

Your rescue dawns like the light in the morning.
    Come and appear, be light to our eyes.

God in the midst of us, flame of our life,
    Come here among us, bring us to life.
God of the powers, God of people,
    Show us your light, bring us to life.

Or are you, God, a God of the dead?
    Come here among us, bring us to life.
Or are you, God, no God of people?
    Show us your light and make us free.

For you are God, light in the morning.
    For you are God, today and tomorrow.
Your covenant will last for a thousand generations.
    For you are God, the God of people.

    All the living are waiting for you.
Open your hand that we may eat our fill.
    Do not turn away, do not let us die.
Do not let us fall back into the dust.
    But send your spirit, and we come to life,
Flame of our life, light of our light—
    Send us your spirit, and we come to life.
Soul of our heart and light of our light,
    Send us your spirit, and we come to life.
Give to this earth the freshness of youth.

    To all your people, everywhere,
To all your people, of every kind,

With that great number beyond all counting
We call to you: Be here among us,
   On this night, be our God,
In this city, be our peace,
   In our houses, give us peace.
On our tables, the bread of peace,
   And for our children, be here among us.

Light in the midst of us, people of peace,
   How long must we go on waiting for you?

Huub Oosterhuis

I N ancient Greek mythology, Prometheus stole fire from the gods and brought it down to those on earth.

This old Greek story is still entertaining and has served to inspire assorted works of genius from poets and artists drawn to a myth, however fanciful, about the origin of fire. More scientifically, archaeologists and anthropologists have much to say about the role that fire played in the process of our evolution. Where would we be now without fire, used from prehistoric times to bring warmth, to cook food, to protect the community, eventually in the first tentative struggles to make a brutal life easier, to create what we now call technology?

And if fire is the magic weapon that we could use to subdue the hostile animal kingdom lurking outside in the darkness, speech is the first accomplishment that would allow us to share more than mere food and warmth with those of our kind huddled together around those prehistoric campsites.

The rituals of our Easter Vigil involve ancient touchstones of human development, first of all with the lighting of the new fire, dramatically accomplished in the pitch dark church, drawing on our most primitive hopes and fears. This is followed by a lengthy liturgy of the word, a tribute to human speech, refined and developed into writing and literature in order to share the history of our thoughts and dreams with our neighbours, over thousands of years of time and uncounted miles of space.

And there's more—after these two timeless fundamentals, we then add the blessing of the Easter water, for water is the most basic need of all living creatures. We can survive for a long time without food; we can last only a few days without water.

Indeed we can go through life without the Light of the World, the Word-made-flesh, or the Living Water, but as seekers of spiritual understanding have always known, we would not be fully alive. And we are thankful on this spring evening to have reached enough of that understanding to be here together in this church, greeting the risen Christ in our hearts and in our lives.

Bertha Catherine Madott

THIS night is to give a new birth to all things; and as the first beginnings of the cosmos did, so this new birth too begins in the sign of light. Light for the church is forever the symbol of the eternal *Logos* of whom the scripture says, "in him was life, and that life was the light of people and the light shines in darkness." Always for her the lighting of the lamps at evening is a flash of this eternal light in the darkness of time, and an invitation to praise God the "unfailing light," the creator of all lights, to praise Christ who is the true bedrock, the fire of God's pure light, like the flame which leaps up from the flint.

For this reason mysteries of light stand at the beginning of this sacred night. In the forecourt of the church we surround the golden spark. The new fire, struck from rock, crackles toward the night sky. The light of earth stands over against the lights of heaven.

The consecration of fire in the Easter night tells Christians that in Christ time has become new; it tells them that with his resurrection the new year of Jubilee, the moments of time, the new *aion,* God's life, has begun. With the joyful procession which brings the new fire into the church, we pass over the step into the new era in the world, God's epoch.

Aemiliana Löhr

Now, O Lord and God, our Savior Jesus Christ, grant spiritual and physical light to our minds and hearts that had been blinded with worldly errors; enlighten us as you enlightened the holy Marys and the holy women who came to your tomb with spices, so they could sprinkle your holy body, the source of life. . . . Since you have raised us up and delivered us from the stain of our sins and the darkness of our transgressions, make us worthy in your loving kindness to kindle our lamps with today's light, the symbol of your radiant and glorious resurrection.

Wisdom! Let us stand! The light of Christ enlightens all people. Blessed be the Father, the Son and the Holy Spirit who enlighten and sanctify our souls and bodies at all times, now and always and for ever and ever.

Byzantine liturgy

Eternal God, in Jesus Christ
you have given the light of life
to all the world.
Sanctify this new fire,
and inflame us with a desire to shine forth
with the brightness of Christ's rising,
until we feast at the banquet of eternal light;
through Jesus Christ, the Sun of Righteousness.

*Book of
Common Worship*

God of life,
through Jesus Christ
you have bestowed upon the world the light of life.
Sanctify this new fire,
and grant that our hearts and minds may also be kindled
with holy desire to shine forth
with the brightness of Christ's rising,
that we may attain to the feast of everlasting life.

*United Methodist
Book of Worship*

I N the beginning was the Word,
and the Word was with God,
and the Word was God.
In him was life,
and the life was the light of all people.
The light shines in the darkness,
and the darkness has not overcome it.

Book of
Common Worship

An acolyte brings the Easter candle to the priest, who cuts a cross in the wax with a stylus. Then the priest traces the Greek letter alpha above the cross, the letter omega below, and the numerals of the current year between the arms of the cross.

C HRIST yesterday and today,
the beginning and the end,
the Alpha
and the Omega.
All time belongs to him
and all the ages.
To him be glory and power
through every age for ever. Amen.

Roman Missal

EITHER the dead are dead,
Or today is eternity,
Your face is eternity,
   Your rays are our endless life.
You are girt with a golden girdle,
   You are with all your crucified
Angels and saints and men
   Who die under clouds in the stars:
You are bringing them back from the dead.
   They breathe on my face as I pray.

Give me your innermost life.
   Come quickly, Alpha, Omega,
Vachel Lindsay   Our God, the beginning and end!

The priest may insert five grains of incense in the candle. He does this in the form of a cross, saying:

By his holy
and glorious wounds
may Christ our Lord
guard us
Roman Missal   and keep us. Amen.

As the center pole of the new creation, the paschal candle is Christ, the Alpha and Omega of all times and ages. It recalls how Jesus appeared to his disciples, displaying his wounds to them and imparting the Spirit to them for the forgiveness of sins. Since the Easter Vigil is popularly taken as a celebration of the resurrection, the candle is understood to represent the risen Christ. Reflection on the various elements that decorate and adorn the candle, however, direct our thoughts to the one who was crucified.

Five wax nails [grains of incense] are inserted into the candle to signify the wounds that Jesus received in his hands, feet and side when he was crucified. "By his holy and glorious wounds, may Christ our Lord guard and keep us." These wounds do not vanish. They remain with Jesus who repeatedly shows them to his disciples. They are offered as marks of recognition: "Look at my hands and my feet; see that it is I myself" (Luke 24:39).

John, more than any other evangelist, attaches importance to Jesus' wounds. He alone mentions the piercing of Jesus' side (John 19:34), and he makes it a major element in the appearance stories of the following week. When Jesus appears to his disciples on the evening of the first day of the week, "he showed them his hands and his side" (John 20:19). Thomas, who was absent on that occasion, protests: "I will never believe it without probing the nailprints in his hands, without putting my finger in the nailmarks and my hand into his side" (John 20:25). Eight days later Jesus commands the doubter: "Take your finger and examine my hands. Put your hand into my side" (John 20:27).

By repeatedly displaying and calling attention to the nailmarks in his hands and especially to his pierced side, Jesus emphasizes the continuity between his present condition and his condition on the cross. It may strike us as strange, initially, but the person who manifests himself to Thomas and the other disciples is the crucified one. He looks no different now than he did on Golgotha; he "is the same yesterday, today and forever" (Hebrews 13:8). What Thomas saw behind locked doors was shown to the whole world on the cross: Jesus Christ lifted up from the earth, filled with glory, pierced with a lance, bestows eternal life on all who believe.

Insofar as the paschal candle with its five nails reflects the thought of John, we must maintain that it is primarily a symbol of the crucified Christ, the pouring out of whose blood is his glorification and our sanctification. As such it strongly evokes the lamb of the book of Revelation who is standing, yet slain (Revelation 5:6), and whose blood is acknowledged as having purchased an entire multitude for God from every race and nation (v. 9). The paschal candle belongs to the tradition which understands the pasch of Jesus to be his passion.

Christ, having allowed Thomas to touch his wounds, urges him, "Do not persist in your unbelief, but believe" (John 20:27). Thomas is not called to believe that Jesus is truly risen. As we have explained, Jesus is portrayed here not as the risen one but as the crucified. Recall the scene at the cross. When Jesus' side was pierced, "immediately blood and water flowed out" (John 19:34). Both blood and water are unmistakable symbols of life. At the very moment of death, the crucified body of Jesus becomes the inexhaustible source of life.

In death Jesus is taken up totally into God. The revelation and communication of God's own self is through his dying. The flow of blood and water from the pierced side invites the beholder to acknowledge Jesus as one in being with God (cf. John 10:30). This is what Thomas beholds. Placing his hand in the hands and side of Jesus, he confesses "My Lord and my God" (John 20:28); he applies the divine names to the crucified one (cf. Psalm 35:23). Thus, the promise of Jesus is fulfilled: "When you lift up the Son of Man, you will come to realize that I AM" (John 8:28).

The paschal candle calls the faithful of every age to share in this confession of Thomas. As a major liturgical sign, the candle functions in the same way the signs do that are recorded in the gospel: "to help you to believe that Jesus is the Messiah, the Son of God, so that through this faith you may have life in his name" (John 20:31).

Patrick Regan

ACCEPT, holy Father, this evening sacrifice of incense. Your ministers offer it to you within this candle, the handiwork of bees, their gift to the church.

Missal of 1570

Lord,
I am not one to despise your gifts.
May you be blessed
who spread the riches of your sweetness
for my zeal. . . .
Let my small span of ardent life
melt into our great communal task;
to lift up to your glory
this temple of sweetness,
a citadel of incense,
a holy candle, myriad-celled,
molded of your graces
and of my hidden work.

The prayer of the bee
Carmen Bernos
de Gasztold

*The Easter candle is lighted from the new fire. The priest may say
the following words:*

May the light of Christ, rising in glory,
dispel the darkness of our hearts and minds.

Roman Missal

Then the deacon takes the Easter candle, lifts it high, and sings alone:

Christ our light.

All answer:

Thanks be to God.

Roman Missal

WHAT can be more appropriate or more merry
than to keep watch for the Flower of Jesse
with this fragrant torch?

Hear how Wisdom sings its praises:
"I am the flower of the field,
    the lily of the valley."
Indeed this wax is the transfigured
    nectar of flowers,

Ambrosian Missal   now made white as snow.

IN the morning sun:
Christ, our light.
In the shining stars:
    Christ, our light.
In the burning bush:
    Christ, our light.
In the pillar of fire:
    Christ, our light.
In the glistening temple:
    Christ, our light.
In the tongues of flame:

Gail Ramshaw   Christ, our light.

LET us go forth in peace!
Missal of 1570   In the name of Christ! Amen.

O house of Jacob,
come, let us walk
in the light of the LORD!

Isaiah 2:5

THE LORD went in front of them in a pillar of cloud by day,
to lead them along the way, and in a pillar of fire by
night, to give them light, so that they might travel by day and
by night.

Exodus 13:21

THE LORD rules: the earth is eager,
joy touches distant lands.
God is wrapped in thunder cloud,
throned on justice, throned on right.

Fire marches out in front
and burns up all resistance.
Overhead, God's lightning flares,
the earth shudders to see it.

Mountains melt down like wax
before the Lord, the ruler of all.
Overhead God's justice resounds,
a glory all people can see.

Psalm 97:1 – 6

*At the church door the deacon lifts the candle high and sings a
second time:*

CHRIST our light.

All answer:

Thanks be to God.

Roman Missal

O N the eve of Easter in the Orthodox churches of Syria and Lebanon (as elsewhere), the congregation follows the priest three times in procession around the church building. Finally the priest approaches the closed doors and chants for the doors to be opened "that the King of Glory may enter."

The doors are thrown open. The church is immediately illuminated and the multitude sings the message of resurrection, *"Al maseeh kam,"* Christ is risen!

Helen Corey

A T last the night of Easter comes with its joyful, exultant sounds. On the stroke of midnight, amidst the flickering of all the candles, a veritable swelling sea of light in the hands of the faithful, the priest and deacon intone the words for which we have waited so long and with such longing to hear: It is the day of the resurrection, let us be illumined! Pasch of the Lord, Pasch! For Christ our God has led us across from death to life, from earth to heaven, that we all should sing the song of victory!

And it grows and rises from a thousand throats, this cry of Easter victory! "Christ has risen from the dead, death overcome by death; he has given life to those who dwelt in tombs." Again and again the verse is sung, made holy by the tremendous mystery it contains, and by centuries of use. It is the finest, the best loved, the best known, the most popular and most familiar formula for the church's transparent joy at Easter.

Nicholas von Arsenief

C OME, O Faithful, and take light from the Light that never fades;
come and glorify Christ who is risen from the dead!

Christ is risen from the dead,
trampling down death by death,
and upon those in the tombs
bestowing life!

Byzantine liturgy

A LL light their candles from the Easter candle and continue in the procession into church.   *Roman Missal*

R EJOICE, rejoice, believers,
and let your lights appear;
the evening is advancing,
and darker night is near.
The bridegroom is arising
and soon is drawing nigh.
Up, pray and watch and wrestle;
at midnight comes the cry.

The watchers on the mountain
proclaim the bridegroom near;
Go forth as he approaches
with glad hosannas clear.
The marriage feast is waiting;
the gates wide open stand.
Arise, O heirs of glory;
the bridegroom is at hand.

Our hope and expectation,
O Jesus, now appear;
Arise, O Sun so longed for,
o'er this benighted sphere.
With hearts and hands uplifted,
we plead, O Lord, to see
The day of earth's redemption   Laurentius Laurentii
that sets your people free!   Seventeenth century

W<small>E</small> now know the magnificence of this pillar,
which sparkles with fire
in your honor.

And even if the fire is divided,
nothing is lost,
nothing is changed.

This precious lamp's mother, the bee,
feeds it herself.

Missal of 1570

I can remember a blustery, rainy Easter night in the Pacific Northwest, where parishioners had witnessed the successful lighting of the Easter fire against all odds. Once inside the church, we felt blessed and victorious with our little flames.

After the services, and after the Easter feastings and greetings were over, we all trekked out to our cars in a blowing rain just trying to get our little flames as far as the car. Two young men approached us from the parking lot and told us they'd gotten all the way to their van, and in slamming the door their candle had gone out. They wanted a share in our flame and wanted to warn us that even closing the car door was a danger to getting our fire home successfully. We shared our flame and crept into our car and sure thing, when we closed the car door, even though we were ever so careful, our candle went out!

Well, the two young men had not driven off yet. They were sitting in their van watching to see how we would fare. Again, they shared their light with us, and we had to laugh with joy and satisfaction at our fire light fraternity. As they drove off, the next family came knocking at our car window needing a light from our candle. We gave them a tip on how to close the car door and save the flame. Up and down the parking lot in the wind and the rain we heard the families laughing and calling out as flames went out and were rekindled. "Wow," said one of our kids, "this fire *is* magic! I know what you mean — you can give it away and you never lose; it only makes more."

Gertrud Mueller
Nelson

When the deacon arrives before the altar, the deacon faces the people and sings a third time:

C<small>HRIST</small> our light.

All answer:

Thanks be to God.

Roman Missal

W<small>E</small> begin the Vigil not with narratives of the resurrection but with a symbol of it: "Christ our light," we say. Darkness we know too well: the toddler's plea that the night-light be left on, the grandpa's terror that he might go blind, the growing depression of the community after days of gray rain or winter's early nightfall. Into such darkness threatening to overwhelm the world comes Christ our light, reversing human fact with divine truth.

When Luke narrates the bestowal of Christ's spirit, he describes on the head of each disciple a tongue as of fire. A paschal flame dances on the head of each of the faithful, as now the fire of God disperses within the community. "Christ our light," we chant. As we watch the candle flicker, not only do we remember the stories of the fire of God, but we also see Christ our light on one another gathered around the fire.

Gail Ramshaw

F<small>IRST</small> only the flame of the Paschal candle, just bright enough to reflect the white silk of the deacon's vestments (what a marvelous joy this sight alone is). . . . Then at the third call of *Lumen Christi:* the blazing up of the hundreds of candles in the hands of the people.

Above all, the young voice of the deacon, trembling with joy, and the incomparable, lovely melody which goes to heaven, sails out over the earth, and sets every heart free with the joy of the Easter news:

> "This is the night.
> O truly blessed night."

"This night," which could bring nothing out of its poor and barren womb except sobs, tears and cries for help, has received the merciful light of God. The light has come down to the dark; although at first it seemed buried in the darkness of night, it overcame this dark, made of the tomb a womb, and leapt out of it once more in a birth of God's life. We people of every age who have come to believe, are this blessed darkness, which may give birth from a barren womb. The light is Christ who gets the victory over our sin as we are baptized, and shines as the morning star within us. This morning star which has no setting rejoices over this night like a mother with her newborn child. This night is changed by this birth, in its very essence light as the day and truly blessed. . . . it has become the night of the Lord's blessed passion and of God's mercy. The place where divine light was buried has given birth to resurrection and a day that shall never end.

It is not a song about events which are over and done with, which have nothing to do with us, but of what is happening now, and what is happening always, when in the course of the year the Pasch returns.

Aemiliana Löhr

Exult and sing, O heav'nly choirs of angels!
Rejoice, all you powers in heaven and on earth!
Jesus Christ our King is risen!
Sound the trumpet, sing of our salvation!

Rejoice, O earth, in shining splendor,
radiant in the brightness of your king!
Lands that once lay covered by darkness,
see Christ's glory filling all the universe!

Rejoice, O mother Church, with all your children,
resplendent in your risen Savior's light!

Let our joyful voices resound this night!
Let God's people shake these walls with shouts of praise!

Rejoice, beloved friends and heirs of Christ,
standing with me in this wondrous light.
Pray that God grant to me, a deacon of the Church,
strength to sing this Easter candle's praises.

The Lord be with you,
And also with you.

Lift up your hearts.
We lift them up to the Lord.

Let us give thanks to the Lord our God.
It is right to give our thanks and praise.

It is truly right and just
that with full hearts and minds and voices,
we should praise you, unseen God, almighty Father,
and your only Son, our Lord Jesus Christ.

For Christ ransomed us with his precious blood
and by nailing to the cross the decree that condemned us,
he paid to you, eternal Father, the price of Adam's sin.

This is our passover feast,
when Christ, the true Lamb, is slain,
whose blood consecrates the homes of all believers.

This is the night
when first you set the children of Israel free:
you saved our ancestors from slavery in Egypt
and led them dry-shod through the sea.

This is the night when you led your people by a pillar of fire:
with your light you showed them the way
and destroyed all the darkness of sin.

This is the night
when Christians everywhere,

washed clean of sin and freed from all defilement,
are restored to grace and grow in holiness.

This is the night
when Jesus Christ broke the chains of death
and in triumphant glory rose from the grave.

What good would life have been for us
had Christ not come as our Redeemer?

O God, how wonderful your care for us!
How boundless your merciful love!
To ransom a slave, you gave up a Son!

O happy fault, O necessary sin of Adam
which gained for us so great a Redeemer!

O night truly blest! O night chosen above all others
to see Christ rise in glory from the dead!

This is the night
of which the Scripture says:

"Even darkness is not dark for you,
and the night will shine as clear as the day!"
How holy is this night,
which heals our wounds and washes all evil away!

A night to restore lost innocence and bring mourners joy!
A night to cast out hatred!
A night for seeking peace and humbling pride!

O truly blessed night
when heaven is wedded to earth
and we are reconciled with God!

Therefore, Father most holy, in the joy of this night,
receive our evening sacrifice of praise,
the solemn offering of your holy people.

Accept this Easter candle,
a flame divided but undimmed,
a pillar of fire that glows to the honor of God.

Let it mingle with the lights of heaven
and continue bravely burning
to dispel the darkness of this night!

May the Morning Star which never sets
find this flame still burning.
Christ is that Morning Star,
who rose to shed his peaceful light on all creation
and lives and reigns with you for ever and ever.
Amen.   *Roman Missal*

THIS candle, a small light in the morning of our paschal liturgy, awaits Christ the Morning Star, that preeminent light transforming all the world's present darkness. Our words, and the words of centuries of the faithful before us, keep vigil through the waiting years by dancing around the fire of this Morning Star, which flickers and blazes, bursts and explodes in our midst. And we say: Surely the fire of God will come to purify the creation; surely the light of God will illumine the present darkness. And we pray: Come, Morning Star, not as the tiny glow we see in the dimmest distance, but as a magnificent burning divine might that, were we close by, could sear our eyesight with the brilliance of mercy. Around the fire we pray: Come, shining Spirit, and kindle in us the fire of your love.   Gail Ramshaw

WHERE can I hide from you?
How can I escape your presence?
I scale the heavens, you are there!
I plunge to the depths, you are there!

If I fly toward the dawn,
or settle across the sea,
even there you take hold of me,
your right hand directs me.

If I think night will hide me
and darkness give me cover,
I find darkness is not dark.
For your night shines like day
darkness and light are one.

You created every part of me,
knitting me in my mother's womb.
For such handiwork, I praise you.
Awesome this great wonder!
Psalm 139:7 – 14   I see it so clearly!

THIS is the paschal feast, the Lord's passing:
so cries the Spirit.
No type or telling, this, no shadow.
Pasch of the Lord it is, and truly.
The blood that is shed is a sign of the blood to be shed,
the first indication of what the Spirit will be,
a glimpse of the great anointing.
"I, seeing the blood, will protect you."

You have indeed protected us, Jesus,
from endless disaster.

You spread your hands like a Father
and fatherlike gave cover with your wings.
Your blood, a God's blood, you poured over the earth,
sealing a blood-bargain for us because you loved us.
You gave us back God's friendship.

The heavens may have your spirit, paradise your soul
but, oh, may the earth have your blood!

This feast of the Spirit
leads the mystic dance through the year.
The Pasch came from God, came from heaven to earth:
from earth it has gone back to heaven.

New is this feast and all-embracing;
all creation assembles at it.

Joy to all creatures, honor, feasting, delight!
Dark death is destroyed
and life is restored everywhere.
The gates of heaven are open.
God has shown himself human,
humanity has gone up to God a god.
The gates of hell are shattered,
the bars of Adam's prison broken.

The people of the world below
have risen from the dead,
bringing good news:
What was promised is fulfilled!
From the earth has come singing and dancing.

This is God's passing!
Heaven's God, showing no meanness,
has joined us together, one with God in the Spirit.
The great marriage hall is full of guests,
all dressed for the wedding,
no guest rejected for want of a wedding dress.

The paschal light is the bright new lamplight,
light that shines from the virgins' lamps.

The light in the soul will never go out.
The fire of grace burns in us all,
spirit, divine, in our bodies and in our souls,
fed with the oil of Christ.

We pray you, God, our Sovereign, Christ,
King for ever in the world of spirits,
stretch out your strong hands over your holy church
and over the people that will always be yours.
Defend, protect, preserve them.
Raise now the sign of victory over us
and grant that we may sing with Moses
the song of triumph.
For yours are victory and power
for ever and ever. Amen.

Attributed to Hippolytus
Third century

Exult and sing, O shining angel choirs!
Exult and dance, bright stars and blazing suns!
The firstborn of creation, Jesus Christ,
is ris'n in radiant splendor from the dead!

Rejoice, O awesome night of our rebirth!
Rejoice, O mother moon, that marks the months!
for from your fullness comes, at last, the Day
when sin is robbed of pow'r and death is slain!

Awaken, earth! Awaken, air and fire!
O children born of clay and water, come!
The One who made you rises like the sun
to scatter night and wipe your tears away.

Arise then, sleepers, Christ enlightens you!
Arise from doubt and sadness, sin and death.
With joyful hearts and spirits set afire,
draw near to sing this Easter candle's praise!

The Lord be with you.
And also with you.

Lift up your hearts.
We lift them up to the Lord.

Let us give thanks to the Lord our God.
It is right to give our thanks and praise.

We praise you, God, for all your works of light!
We bless you for that burst of fire and flame
through which you first created all that is:
a living universe of soaring stars,
of space and spinning planets, surging seas
that cradle earth and rock against her breast.

We praise you, God of everlasting light!

We praise you for light's beauty, motion, speed:
for eastern light that paints the morning sky,
for western light that slants upon our doors,
inviting us to praise you ev'ry night.

We praise you, God of everlasting light!

We bless you for the light invisible:
the fire of faith, the Spirit's grace and truth,
the light that bonds the atom, stirs the heart
and shines for ever on the face of Christ!

We praise you, God of everlasting light!

Creator, in the joy of Easter eve,
accept our off'ring of this candle's light:
may all who see its glow and feel its warmth
be led to know your nature and your Name.

We praise you, God of everlasting light!

For, Father, it was your own light and love
that led your people Israel dryshod
through foaming seas, and brought them safe at last
to lands of milk and honey. In your love

you led them as a shining cloud by day,
and as a flaming shaft of fire by night.

This is the night, most blessed of all nights,
when first you rescued people from the sea:
a sign of that new birth which was to come
in blood and water flowing from Christ's side.

Now is Christ risen! We are raised with him!

This is the night, most blessed of all nights,
when your creating Spirit stirred again
to turn back chaos and renew the world,
redeeming it from hatred, sin and strife.

Now is Christ risen! We are raised with him!

This is the night, most blessed of all nights,
when all the powers of heaven and earth were wed
and every hungry human heart was fed
by Christ our Lamb's own precious flesh and blood.

Now is Christ risen! We are raised with him!

O night, more holy than all other nights,
your watchful eyes beheld, in wondrous awe,
the triumph of our Savior over sin,
the rising of the Deathless One from death!

Now is Christ risen! We are raised with him!

O night that gave us back what we had lost!
O night that made our sin a happy fault!
Beyond our deepest dreams this night, O God,
your hand reached out to raise us up in Christ.

Now is Christ risen! We are raised with him!

O night of endless wonder, night of bliss,
when every living creature held its breath
as Christ robbed death and harrowed hopeless hell,
restoring life to all those in the tomb!

Now is Christ risen! We are raised with him!

And so, our God, Creator of all life,
with open hearts and hands we come to you:
anointed with the Spirit's pow'r, we bear
these precious, glowing gifts of fire and flame.

We pray that when our night of watching ends,
the Morning Star who dawns and never sets,
our Savior Jesus Christ, may find us all
united in one faith, one hope, one Lord.

For you alone are God, living and true:
all glory, praise, and pow'r belong to you
with Jesus Christ, the One who conquered death,
and with the Spirit blest for ever more.

Amen.   *Roman Missal*

L ET us rise in early morning,
   And, instead of ointments, bring
Hymns of praises to our Master,
   And his resurrection sing:
We shall see the Sun of Justice
   Ris'n with healing on his wing.

Rescued by your loving kindness
   From their exile's misery,
Now the righteous rise to hasten
   Toward the far-off light they see,

Weave the dance that leads to Pascha,
Raise the song of victory!

Go forth then, you saints, to meet him!
Go with lamps in every hand!
From the sepulchre he rises:
Ready for the Bridegroom stand:
Hail the Pascha of salvation
With his friends from ev'ry land!

John of Damascus
Eighth century

Oglistening starlight,
O elect, resplendent,
and royal bride,
O sparkling gem:
you are arrayed as a noble dame
without spot or wrinkle,
you are a companion of angels,
a fellow citizen with saints.
Flee, flee the ancient destroyer's
cave and come—
come into the palace of the King!

Hildegard of Bingen
Twelfth century

THE paschal night is in a very special sense the church's bridal feast. All the bridal and marriage images which have accompanied us full of promise since the Epiphany find their completion today. The image of Jacob's well has found its reality. The woman who had no husband, yet belonged to many, has found once more the only spouse she was meant by God to have. Humanity, for whom alone the call is meant, at last recognizes that it had turned itself to one who is faithless and a deceiver: "My spouse, I greet you; hear my greeting, young light." There is only one light; there is only one spouse; Christ has received the honor of this name. Here in the night of Easter, from the church's mouth the ancient cry of the mysteries awakens to its real meaning in the presence of the light of the paschal candle, the image of Christ. It is night; the bridegroom is here. He comes to the house of his betrothed, and he finds her watching. She has not slept all the while he was in the tomb. Now he has come back, alive. His locks stream the dew of the night. He still bears on his body the marks of his pain; but he has grown into the more than human, into the glorious body; clothed in Godhead he "stands before the door, looks through the window, peeps through the blinds." Until now she has only seen him through the window and blinds of the prophets' dark sayings and images. Now he has walked in from the night's dark pass, and overpowered every image and every prophecy with the glory of his resurrection.   Aemiliana Löhr

O night that was my guide!
   Oh darkness dearer than the morning's pride,
Oh night that joined the lover
To the beloved bride
Transfiguring them each into the other.

Lost to myself I stayed
My face upon my lover having laid
From all endeavour ceasing;
And all my cares releasing   John of the Cross
Threw them amongst the lilies there to fade.   Sixteenth century

ONE of these nights about twelve o'clock,
The old world's a-gonna to reel and rock,
The sinner's gonna tremble and cry for pain
And the Lord will come in his aeroplane.

You will have to get ready if you take this ride,
Quit all your sins and humble your pride,
You must furnish a lamp both bright and clean
And a vessel of oil to run the machine.

When our journey is over and we'll all sit down
At the marriage supper with a robe and crown,
We'll blend our voices with the heavenly throng
And praise our Savior as the years roll on.

Oh, ye thirsty of every tribe,
Get your ticket for an aeroplane ride,
Jesus our Savior is a-coming to reign
Ozark folk song   And take you up to glory in his aeroplane.

THEREFORE doth it behoove the church to await, with sweet lights, the coming of the Spouse, and with all possible devotion to weigh the holy gift it has received. Holy vigils, such as this, should have no fellowship with darkness. We should be wise, and make the light of our lamp be unceasing; lest, while we are preparing to trim it with oil, our Lord should come and we be too late to do him homage, for we are assured that he will come in the twinkling of the eye, as a flash of light.

Therefore, this day's evening is rich in the fullness of the most august mysteries, which, though prefigured or accomplished at various times, are all brought before us during the course of this night. For firstly, we have this evening torch, which leads the way, as did the star that guided the Magi. Then follows the font of spiritual regeneration, as it were the river of Jordan, in which our Lord vouchsafed to be baptised. Thirdly we have the priest's apostolic words announcing the resurrection of Christ. Then, to complete the mysteries, the faithful flock feeds on the flesh of Christ. May this flock enjoy the day of our Lord's resurrection!

Ambrosian Missal

IN the secret and the darkness of this night,
you, our God, have embraced us,
thrown aside the whole past to love your world for ever.
This is the wedding night of the church,
and this great hall is our bridal chamber.
Pledge yourself to us
and to those who will tonight be baptized.
Pledge a love that will lead us in ways of justice,
in the very way of our Lord Jesus Christ.

Gabe Huck

FRIENDS in Christ,
let us listen attentively to the word of God,
recalling God's saving deeds throughout history
and how, in the fullness of time,
God's word became flesh and dwelt among us:
Jesus Christ, our Redeemer!

*Book of
Common Worship*

HEAR me, heaven and earth,
listen to what I say.
May my thoughts fall like rain,
may my words cling like dew,
like gentle rain upon tender grass,
like showers upon seedlings.
I will praise the Lord's name,
I will tell of God's greatness.

Deuteronomy 32:1 – 3

WE have no mythology in Judaism, only history, only
memory. So I *must* be able to see Abraham, Isaac,
Jacob, and I *must* be able to see Joseph.

Elie Wiesel

IT is memory that is the somnambulist. It will come back in
its wounds from across the world . . . calling us by our
names and demanding its rightful tears. It will never be
impervious. The memory can be hurt, time and again — but
in that may lie its final mercy. As long as it's vulnerable to
the living moment, it lives for us, and while it lives, and
while we are able, we can give it up its due.

Eudora Welty

B OTH academic and fundamentalist interpreters who deal with the scriptural text apart from its communal origins, its meaning and its relation to present church formation abuse that text. Scripture is rightly read and interpreted within the liturgy, which keeps reminding us of the whole story of God.

Stanley Hauerwas
William B. Willimon

F OR Christians, the religion of the Bible is an uninterrupted "creation" of the cosmos — and it is in scripture that they claim to have read it. The Father of our Lord Jesus Christ works without cease. It is a religion of movement because, from the oak of Mamre to the burning bush, from Sinai to the dedication of the temple, its manifestations come in series; it is progressive because it is made up of promises which give upon an indefinite future. From stage to stage it moves through a landscape which renews itself, never becoming static. Not that the present abolishes the past; it uses the past in bringing it to perfection, without cease it recalls the past to justify itself and meanwhile it already evokes the future. Truly, the biblical religion is a dynamic religion, never complacent, ever magnifying its God, the indefectible Creator. Enough to say that in the name of the freedom of the Spirit of God, the religion of the Bible, confronting the partisans of the past, wears the guise of opposition and contradiction. And this is the way the prophets understood it.

Hilaire Duesberg

WHEN we talk about the writer's country we are liable to forget that no matter what particular country it is, it is inside as well as outside him. Art requires a delicate adjustment of the outer and inner worlds in such a way that, without changing their nature, they can be seen through each other. To know oneself is to know one's region. It is also to know the world, and it is also, paradoxically, a form of exile from that world. The writer's value is lost, both to himself and to his country, as soon as he ceases to see that country as a part of himself, and to know oneself is, above all, to know what one lacks. It is to measure oneself against truth, and not the other way around. The first product of self-knowledge is humility, and this is not a virtue conspicuous in any national character.

Saint Cyril of Jerusalem, in instructing catechumens, wrote: "The dragon sits by the side of the road, watching those who pass. Beware lest he devour you. We go to the Father of Souls, but it is necessary to pass by the dragon." No matter what form the dragon may take, it is of this mysterious passage past him, or into his jaws, that stories of any depth will always be concerned to tell, and this being the case, it requires considerable courage at any time, in any country, not to turn away from the storyteller.

Flannery O'Connor

W HAT it really comes down to is that we all approach this night *demanding* to hear these stories — because we know that this is the night they happen in front of our eyes. Standing with us this night are all the people of these stories, our ancestors. After hearing how God delivered Daniel, how God freed the Hebrews, how God set the spangled stars in the sky, we come to hear the gospel of resurrection not with confusion or even surprise but rather with a confident "of course!"   Peter Mazar

L ET those saved by God
tell their story:
how the Lord snatched them
from the oppressor's might,
gathering them from east and west,
from north and south.   Psalm 107:2–3

P ERHAPS I should write like the scribes of the Anglo-Saxon Chronicle, saying in the same breath that an archbishop passed away, a synod was held and fiery dragons were seen flying in the air. Why not, after all? Beliefs are relative. Our connection with reality is always tenuous. . . . In the frozen stone of the cathedrals of Europe there co-exist the apostles, Christ and Mary, lambs, fish, gryphons, dragons, sea-serpents and the faces of men with leaves for hair. I approve of that liberality of mind.   Penelope Lively

ALL the days of the year Balaam's talking donkey may be a mere fairy tale, but not on the Sabbath wherein this portion is read in the synagogue, when it speaks to me out of the open Torah. But if not a fairy tale, what then? I cannot say right now; if I should think about it today, when it is past, and try to say what it is, I should probably only utter the platitude that it is a fairy tale. But on that day, in that very hour, it is — well, certainly not a fairy tale, but that which is communicated to me provided I am able to fulfill the command of the hour, namely, to open my ears.

Franz Rosenzweig

GOD of mercy,
on this one night in all the year
we come together hungry and thirsty.
Over and over again we open the book of scripture
to devour your word,
to quench our thirst with your word.
Then let your words be on our lips
when we rise up and when we lie down,
when we are in our homes
and when we go on our way.

Gabe Huck

O dying souls, behold your living spring;
O dazzled eyes, behold your sun of grace;
Dull ears, attend what word this Word doth bring;
Up, heavy hearts, with joy your joy embrace.

Robert Southwell
Sixteenth century

From death, from dark, from deafness, from despairs,
This life, this light, this Word, this joy repairs.

COME, Holy Ghost, our hearts inspire,
   let us thine influence prove,
source of the old prophetic fire,
   fountain of life and love.

Come Holy Ghost (for moved by thee
   the prophets wrote and spoke),
unlock the truth, thyself the key,
   unseal the sacred book.

Expand thy wings, Celestial Dove,
   brood o'er our nature's night;
on our disordered spirits move,
   and let there now be light.

Charles Wesley
Eighteenth century

WE read in the sacramentary that "it must always be borne in mind that the reading of the word of God is the fundamental element of the Easter Vigil." The celebration of the sacraments of initiation may be the center of the night's liturgy, but the scripture reading is the foundation. The structure of this service has each reading followed by a collect, very often with a psalm or canticle and period of silence between the two. The list of readings has varied from one tradition to another, from one century to another, but certain texts occur again and again: the creation, Abraham and Isaac, the exodus, Jonah, passages from Isaiah, the vision of the dry bones, the story of the three young men from Daniel. The lists found in the present liturgical books reflect the various strands of our tradition. In the chart that follows, the scriptures are listed in the order in which they are read. Psalms and canticles are given in parentheses.

Gabe Huck

Roman (Middle Ages to 1955)	Roman (Current)	Lutheran Book of Worship
Gn 1:1 — 2:2 *The days of creation*	Gn 1:1 — 2:2 (Psalm 104:1 – 2, 5 – 6, 10, 12 – 14, 24, 35 *or* Psalm 33:4 – 7, 12 – 13, 20, 22)	Gn 1:1 — 2:2 *or* 1:1 — 3:24
Gn 5:32 — 6:22; 7:6, 11 – 14, 18 – 24; 8:1 – 3, 6 – 12, 15 – 21 *Noah and the flood*		Gn 7:1 – 5, 11 – 18; 8:6 – 18; 9:8 – 13
Gn 22:1 – 19 *Abraham and Isaac*	Gn 22:1 – 18 (Psalm 16:5, 8 – 11)	Gn 22:1 – 18
Ex 14:24 — 15:1 *Crossing the Red Sea*	Ex 14:15 — 15:1 (Ex 15:1 – 6, 17 – 18)	Ex 14:10 — 15:1 *or* 13:17 — 15:1 (Ex 15:1 – 2, 6, 11, 13, 17)
The tender and eternal love of the Lord	Is 54:5 – 14 (Psalm 30:1, 3 – 5, 10 – 12)	
Is 54:17 — 55: 11 *The everlasting covenant*	Is 55:1 – 11 (Is 12:2 – 6)	Is 55:1 – 11
Bar 3:9 – 38 *Praise of wisdom*	Bar 3:9 – 15, 32; 4:1 – 4 (Psalm 19:7 – 1)	Bar 3:9 – 37
Sprinkling of clean water	Ez 36:16 – 28 (Psalm 42:2, 4; 43:3, 4 *or* Is 12:2 – 6 *or* Psalm 51:10 – 13, 16 – 17)	
Ez 37:1 – 14 *Vision of the dry bones*		Ez 37:1 – 14
Is 4:1 – 6 (Is 5:1 – 2) *The Lord's glory, our shelter and shade*		Is 4:2 – 6 (Is 5:1 – 2, 7)
Ex 12:1 – 11 *The Passover ritual*		Ex 12:1 – 14 *or* 12:1 – 24
Jon 3:1 – 10 *Repentance of Nineveh*		Jon 3:1 – 10
Dt 31:22 – 30 (Dt 32:1 – 4) *The song of Moses*		Dt 31:19 – 30 (Dt 32:1 – 4, 7, 36, 43)
Dn 3:1 – 24 *The three young men in the fiery furnace*		Dn 3:1 – 29 (Dn 3:57 – 87)
The Lord gathering the remnant		

Book of Common Prayer	Revised Common Lectionary	Byzantine Tradition
Gn 1:1 — 2:2 (Psalm 33:1 – 11 or Psalm 36:5 – 10)	Gn 1:1 – 2:4a (Psalm 136:1 – 9, 23 – 26)	Gn 1:1 – 14
Gn 7:1 – 5, 11 – 18; 8:6 18; 9:8 – 13 (Psalm 46)	Gn 7:1 – 5, 11 – 18; 8:6 – 18; 9:8 – 13 (Psalm 46)	
Gn 22:1 – 18 (Psalm 33:12 – 22 or Psalm 16)	Gn 22:1 – 18 (Psalm 16)	
Ex 14:10 — 15:1 (Ex 15:1 – 6, 11 – 13, 17 – 18)	Ex 14; 10 – 31; 15:20 – 21 (Ex 15:1b – 13, 17 – 18)	Ex 13:20 — 15:19
Is 55:1 – 11 (Is 12:2 – 6 or Psalm 42:1 – 7)	Is 55:1 – 11 (Is 12:2 – 6)	
	Bar 3:9 – 15, 32 – 4:4 or: Proverbs 8:1 – 8, 19 – 21; 9:4b – 6 (Psalm 19)	
Ez 36:24 – 28 (Psalm 42:1 – 7 or Is 12:2 – 6)	Ez 36:24 – 28 (Psalm 42 and 43)	
Ez 37:1 – 14 (Psalm 30 or Psalm 143)	Ez 37:1 – 14 (Psalm 143)	Ez 37:1 – 14
Is 4:2 – 6* (Psalm 122)		
		Ex 12:1 – 11
		Jon (entire)
		Dn 3:1 – 56
Zep 3:12 – 20 (Psalm 98 or Psalm 126)	Zep 3:14 – 20 (Psalm 98)	Zep 3:8 – 15†

* This reading precedes Isaiah 55.
† The Byzantine tradition also includes the following: Is 60:1 – 16; Jos 5:10 – 15; 1 Kgs 17:8 – 24; Is 61:10 — 62:5; Gn 22:1 – 18; Is 61:1 – 9; 2 Kgs 4:8 – 37; Is 63:11 — 64:5; Jer 31:31 – 34.

I N the beginning when God created the heavens and the earth, the earth was a formless void and darkness covered the face of the deep, while a wind from God swept over the face of the waters. Then God said, "Let there be light"; and there was light. And God saw that the light was good; and God separated the light from the darkness. God called the light Day, and the darkness God called Night. And there was evening and there was morning, the first day.

Genesis 1:1 – 5

H OW wondrous great,
how glorious bright must our Creator be,
who dwells amidst the dazzling light
of vast eternity.

Our soaring spirits upward rise
unto the burning throne.
There would we see the blessed Three
and the almighty One.

Our reason stretches all its wings,
and climbs above the skies.
But still how far beneath God's feet
our mortal knowledge lies!

While all the heav'nly pow'rs conspire
eternal praise to bring,
let faith in humble notes adore,
the glorious Myst'ry sing.

Isaac Watts
Eighteenth century

DAY is a literal translation; night is a poetic translation.   Andrei Codrescu

LIKE a mighty wind over waters
your spirit rushed about the chaos,
God of darkness and of light.
Day by day you labored
and day by day you found your work good.
Then on the sixth day you made the holy parents of us all,
Adam and Eve,
who on this night rejoiced —
as we in this church rejoice —
to see the gates of death broken down
and all the power of evil trampled
by our Lord Jesus Christ,
who lives and reigns with you, one God,
for ever and ever.   Gabe Huck

G OD said, "Let there be a dome in the midst of the waters, and let it separate the waters from the waters." So God made the dome and separated the waters that were under the dome from the waters that were above the dome. And it was so. God called the dome Sky. And there was evening and there was morning, the second day.

God said, "Let the waters under the sky be gathered together into one place, and let the dry land appear." And it was so. God called the dry land Earth, and the waters that were gathered together he called Seas. And God saw that it was good. Then God said, "Let the earth put forth vegetation: plants yielding seed, and fruit trees of every kind on earth that bear fruit with the seed in it." And it was so. The earth brought forth vegetation: plants yielding seed of every kind, and trees of every kind bearing fruit with the seed in it. And God saw that it was good. And there was evening and there was morning, the third day.

And God said, "Let there be lights in the dome of the sky to separate the day from the night; and let them be for signs and for seasons and for days and years, and let them be lights in the dome of the sky to give light upon the earth." And it was so. God made the two great lights — the greater light to rule the day and the lesser light to rule the night — and the stars. God set them in the dome of the sky to give light upon the earth, to rule over the day and over the night, and to separate the light from the darkness. And God saw that it was good. And there was evening and there was morning, the

Genesis 1:6 – 19   fourth day.

T HE sky tells the glory of God,
tells the genius of God's work.
Day carries the news to day,
night brings the message to night,

without a word, without a sound,
without a voice being heard,
yet their message fills the world,
their news reaches its rim.

There God has pitched a tent
for the sun to rest and rise renewed
like a bridegroom rising from bed,
an athlete eager to run the race.

It springs from the edge of the earth,
runs a course across the sky
to win the race at heaven's end.
Nothing on earth escapes its heat.   Psalm 19:2–7

GRATITUDE to Mother Earth,
sailing through night and day—
and to her soil: rich, rare and sweet
in our minds so be it.

Gratitude to Plants, the sun-facing light-changing leaf
and fine root-hairs; standing still through wind and rain;
their dance is in the flowing spiral grain
in our minds so be it.

Gratitude to Air, bearing the soaring Swift and the silent
Owl at dawn. Breath of our song
clear spirit breeze
in our minds so be it.

Gratitude to Water: clouds, lakes, rivers, glaciers;
holding or releasing; streaming through all
our bodies salty seas
in our minds so be it.

Gratitude to the Sun: blinding pulsing light through
trunks of trees, through mists, warming caves where

bears and snakes sleep — he who wakes us —
in our minds so be it.

Gratitude to the Great Sky
who holds billions of stars — and goes yet beyond that —
beyond all powers, and thoughts
and yet is within us —
Grandfather Space.
The mind is his wife.

Mohawk prayer   *So be it.*

Peoples of the earth,
    you who swathe yourselves
with the force of the unknown
constellations as with rolls of thread,
you who sew and sever what is sewn,
you who enter the tangle of tongues
as into beehives,
to sting the sweetness
and be stung —

Peoples of the earth,
do not destroy the universe of words,
let not the knife of hatred lacerate
the sound born together with the first breath.

Peoples of the earth,
O that no one mean death when he says life —
and not blood when he speaks cradle —

Peoples of the earth,
leave the words at their source,
for it is they that can nudge

the horizons into the true heaven
and that, with night gaping behind
their averted side, as behind a mask,
help give birth to the stars —

Nelly Sachs

G OD fixes the number of stars,
calling each by name.
Great is our God and powerful,
wise beyond all telling.

Psalm 147:4 – 5

G OD said, "Let the waters bring forth swarms of living
creatures, and let birds fly above the earth across the
dome of the sky." So God created the great sea monsters and
every living creature that moves, of every kind, with which
the waters swarm, and every winged bird of every kind. And
God saw that it was good. God blessed them, saying, "Be
fruitful and multiply and fill the waters in the seas, and let
birds multiply on the earth." And there was evening and
there was morning, the fifth day.

Genesis 1:20 – 23

Q UESTION the beauty of the earth, question the beauty of
the sea, question the beauty of the air distending and
diffusing itself, question the beauty of the sky . . . question
all these realities. All respond: "See, we are beautiful." Their
beauty is a profession. [But] these beauties are subject to
change. Who made them if not the Beautiful One, who is
not subject to change?

Augustine
Fifth century

I stood and looked and heard the song of the world that told of the splendor of itself, like an object created by all that happened in it, and of what was done in it through all its years: it sang out in voice frail and trembling of fallings of angels, down from a red raging heaven like falling birds or leaves or dropped flowers; of the first man and woman naked and yawning in a garden, their flesh speaking (O for some intimacy of bodies speaking to each other, creating a language for the first time that would be the speech of all love in all the years — one simple sentence of touch and burst) a language that would create and speak out into the world all passion and all despair, loneliness for lack of it that would be a kind of dumbness of speech — where there is no love there is no speech — and desire like speech unheard, and ecstasy like the murmuring and pouring out of the sentence, bring body to body and start a ceaseless murmuring, the turning of the wheel of blood, yearning and tiring and yearning again, eternally rising and falling. And the song sang of kings and falls of kings, and plots of princes; princesses in grated towers and queens in love or sending out ships or causing battles for nations, and conquests of religions and building of stained jewels of churches; of classes, riots and clashes of classes, and systems discovered by one man for all ages, and laws and pacts and edicts. The singing was of architecture of great stone buildings standing in light and throwing down their shadows across swept spacious plazas, and of figures on the capitals of columns — doves and granite grapes and tongued gargoyles; of painted and striped baubles of cities, glittering with loot of robbed wealth, built over water, built on mountainsides; of palaces and great dynastic houses and fortifications and monasteries.

William Goyen

THIS earth with its store of wonders untold,
  Almighty thy power hath founded of old;
hath 'stablished it fast by a changeless decree,
and round it hath cast, like a mantle, the sea.

Thy bountiful care what tongue can recite?
It breathes in the air, it shines in the light;
it streams from the hills, it descends to the plain,
and sweetly distills in the dew and the rain.

Robert Grant
Nineteenth century

GOD said, "Let the earth bring forth living creatures
  according to their kinds; cattle and creeping things and
beasts of the earth according to their kinds." And it was so.
And God made the beasts of the earth according to their
kinds and the cattle according to their kinds, and everything
that creeps upon the ground according to its kind. And God
saw that it was good.

Then God said, "Let us make humankind in our image,
according to our likeness; and let them have dominion over
the fish of the sea, and over the birds of the air, and over the
cattle, and over all the wild animals of the earth, and over
every creeping thing that creeps upon the earth."

So God created humankind in the divine image; in the image
of God humankind was created; male and female God created them.

God blessed them, and God said to them, "Be fruitful and
multiply, and fill the earth and subdue it; and have dominion over the fish of the sea and over the birds of the air and
over every living thing that moves upon the earth." God
said, "See, I have given you every plant yielding seed which
is upon the face of all the earth, and every tree with seed in
its fruit; you shall have them for food. And to every beast of

the earth, and to every bird of the air, and to everything that creeps on the earth, everything that has the breath of life, I have given every green plant for food." And it was so. God saw everything that had been made, and indeed, it was very good. And there was evening and there was morning, the sixth day.

Thus the heavens and the earth were finished, and all their multitude.

Genesis 1:24—2:1

Wᴴᴱɴ I with pleasing Wonder stand,
And all my Frame survey,
Lord, 'tis thy Work, I own; thy Hand
Thus built my humble Clay.

Our Life contains a thousand Springs,
And dies, if one be gone:
Strange! that a Harp, of thousand Strings,
Should keep in Tune so long.

The Continental
Harmony

Tʜᴇ very beginning of Genesis tells us that God created people in order to give them dominion over fish and fowl and all creatures. Of course, Genesis was written by a human, not a horse. . . . Perhaps a man hitched to the cart of a Martian . . . will recall the veal cutlet he used to slice on his dinner plate and apologize (belatedly!) to the cow. . . .

Tereza keeps appearing before my eyes. I see her sitting on the stump petting her sick dog Karenin's head and ruminating human debacles. Another image also comes to mind: Nietzsche leaving his hotel in Turin. Seeing a horse and a workman beating it with a whip, Nietzsche went up to the horse and, before the coachman's very eyes, put his arms around the horse's neck and burst into tears. . . . Nietzsche was trying to apologize to the horse for Descartes. His lunacy (that is, his final break with humankind) began at the very moment he burst into tears over the horse.

And that is the Nietzsche I love, just as I love Tereza with the mortally ill dog resting his head in her lap. I see them one next to the other: both stepping down from the road along which "the master and proprietor of nature" marches onward.   Milan Kundera

I will bless you, Lord my God!
You fill the world with awe.
You dress yourself in light,
in rich, majestic light.

You stretched the sky like a tent,
built your house beyond the rain.
You ride upon the clouds,
the wind becomes your wings,
the storm becomes your herald,
your servants, bolts of light.

You made the earth solid,
fixed it for good.
You made the sea a cloak,
covering hills and all.

At your command
the sea fled your thunder,
swept over mountains,
down the valleys to its place.
You set its limits,
never to drown the earth again.

You feed springs that feed brooks,
rushing down ravines,

water for wild beasts,
for wild asses to drink.
Birds nest nearby
and sing among the leaves.

You drench the hills
with rain from high heaven.
You nourish the earth
with what you create.

You make grass grow for cattle,
make plants grow for people,
food to eat from the earth
and wine to warm the heart,
oil to glisten on faces
and bread for bodily strength.

In Lebanon God planted trees,
the flourishing cedar.
Sparrows nest in the branches,
the stork in treetops.
High crags for wild goats,
rock holes for badgers.

Your moon knows when to rise,
your sun when to set.
Your darkness brings on night
when wild beasts prowl.
The young lions roar to you
in search of prey.

They slink off to dens
to rest at daybreak,
then people rise to work
until the daylight fades.

God, how fertile your genius!
You shape each thing,
you fill the world
with what you do.

I watch the sea, wide and deep,
filled with fish, large and small,
with ships that ply their trade,
and your own toy, Leviathan.

All look to you for food
when they hunger;
you provide it and they feed.
You open your hand, they feast;
you turn away, they fear.

You steal their breath,
they drop back into dust.
Breathe into them, they rise;
the face of the earth comes alive!

Let God's glory endure
and the Lord delight in creating.
One look from God, earth quivers;
one touch, and mountains erupt.

I will sing to my God,
make music for the Lord
as long as I live.
Let my song give joy to God
who is a joy to me.

Psalm 104:1 – 34

S HOUT joy to the Lord,
lovers of justice,
how right to praise!
Praise God on the harp,
with ten-string lyre
sing to the Lord.

Sing God a new song.
Play music to match
your shout of joy.

For the word of the Lord is true:
what God says, God does.
This lover of truth and justice
fills the earth with love.

God speaks: the heavens are made;
God breathes: the stars shine.
God bottles the waters of the sea
and stores them in the deep.

All earth, be astounded,
stand in awe of God.
God speaks: the world is;
God commands: all things appear.

God blocks the plans of nations,
Disrupts all they contrive.
But God's plan and designs
last from age to age.
Blest the land whose god is the Lord,
the heirs whom God has chosen.

The Lord looks down
and sees our human kind.
From heaven God surveys
all peoples on earth.
The maker of human hearts
knows every human act.

Armies do not save kings,
brute force does not spare soldiers.
The warhorse is a sham;
despite its power, it will not save.

God keeps a loving eye
on all who believe,
on those who count on God
to bring relief from famine,
to rescue them from death.

With all we are, we wait for God,
the Lord, our help, our shield.
Our hearts find joy in the Lord;
we trust God's holy name.   ✦
Love us, Lord!
We wait for you.   *Psalm 33*

Oh God, who wonderfully created, and yet more wonderfully restored, the dignity of human nature: Grant that
we may share the divine life of him who humbled himself to   *Book of*
share our humanity, your Son Jesus Christ our Lord.   *Common Prayer*

Almighty and eternal God,
how wonderful is the work of your creation,
how wisely you establish all things in order!
Enlighten the people you have saved,
that we may perceive
the greater wonder of your new creation,
brought forth in the fullness of time,
when Christ our Passover was sacrificed.   *Roman Missal*

THEN the LORD said to Noah, "Go into the ark, you and all your household, for I have seen that you alone are righteous before me in this generation. Take with you seven pairs of all clean animals, the male and its mate; and a pair of the animals that are not clean, the male and its mate; and seven pairs of the birds of the air also, male and female, to keep their kind alive on the face of all the earth. For in seven days I will send rain on the earth for forty days and forty nights; and every living thing that I have made I will blot out from the face of the ground." And Noah did all that the LORD had commanded him.

In the six hundredth year of Noah's life, in the second month, on the seventeenth day of the month, on that day all the fountains of the great deep burst forth, and the windows of the heavens were opened. The rain fell on the earth forty days and forty nights. On the very same day Noah with his sons, Shem and Ham and Japheth, and Noah's wife and the three wives of his sons entered the ark, they and every wild animal of every kind, and all the domestic animals of every kind, and every creeping thing that creeps on the earth, and every bird of every kind — every bird, every winged creature. They went into the ark with Noah, two and two of all flesh in which there was the breath of life. And those that entered, male and female of all flesh, went in as God had commanded him; and the LORD shut him in.

The flood continued forty days on the earth; and the waters increased, and bore up the ark, and it rose high above the earth. The waters swelled and increased greatly on the earth; and the ark floated on the face of the waters.

Genesis 7:1 – 5, 11 – 18

WAIT, my soul, silent for God,
for God alone, my hope,
alone my rock, my safety,
my refuge: I stand secure.

God is my glory and safety,
my stronghold, my haven.
People, give your hearts to God,
trust always! God is our haven.   Psalm 62:6 – 9

IN order that we may know the events of the day of Noah,
Let us listen to the words of the scripture
For the Lover of all spoke clearly to Noah when He saw
        the wickedness of the people of old.

"A critical time for all humankind has come to my attention,
    For earth is full of every kind of evil;
Now I shall bring them and all their offspring to ruin
    To eradicate sin,
    Since all things are full of corruption.
Of all their race, you are the one and only person
    Who is just and pleasing in my sight; you have flourished
In the manner of a rose among thorns. So, heed my words,
    To bring my will as you cry to me:
    'Save all from thy anger, through thy love for us,
        redeemer of all.'

"Obtain, then, some logs of wood that have not rotted,
    And you will make an ark just as I wish it to be,
    Of the kind that I shall show you so that it will bear,
    as in a womb, the seeds of future races.
And, make it like a house in the image of the church,
    In the proportions that I dictate to you.

"You will make the birds' nests and, having strengthened
        the ark with tar,

Build it three hundred cubits in length
By fifty in width."

Noah speaks:
"O my God, formerly thou has brought me forth
      from my mother;
   Save me also in this good ark.
I am shut up in it as in a tomb;
   From it, I shall come forth through thy power
   Just as from a tomb at thy command.
In it, I shall be the prototype of the resurrection
      common to all,
   In which thou art to save the just from fire,
      as thou dost save
Me from the midst of the impious,
   Snatching me away in the ocean of evil."

Romanos
Sixth century

I believe,
Lord, I believe!
It is faith that saves us, you have said it!
I believe the world was made for me,
because as it dies
I thrive on it.
My undertaker's black
is in keeping with my cynical old heart.
Raven land is between you
and that life down there, for whose end I wait
to gratify myself.
"Aha!" I cry, *"Avant moi de déluge!"*
What a feast!
I shall never go back to the Ark!
To the Ark . . .
Oh! let it die in me—
this horrible nostalgia.

The prayer of the raven
Carmen Bernos
de Gasztold

S ING thanks to the Lord,
sound the harp for our God.
The Lord stretches the clouds,
sending rain to the earth,
clothing mountains with green.

The Lord feeds the cattle
and young ravens when they call.   Psalm 147:7–9

L IKE Noah's weary dove, that soared the earth around,
but not a resting place above the cheerless waters found;

O cease, my wandering soul, on restless wing to roam.
All the wide world to either pole has not for thee a home.

Behold the ark of God, behold the open door.
Hasten to gain that dear abode, and rove, my soul,
William A.
Mühlenberg
   no more.   Nineteenth century

A LMIGHTY God, you have placed in the skies the sign of
your covenant with all living things: Grant that we, who
are saved through water and the Spirit, may worthily offer to   *Book of*
you our sacrifice of thanksgiving.   *Common Prayer*

At the end of forty days Noah opened the window of the ark that he had made and sent out the raven; and it went to and fro until the waters were dried up from the earth. Then he sent out the dove from him to see if the waters had subsided from the face of the ground; but the dove found no place to set its foot, and it returned to him to the ark, for the waters were still on the face of the whole earth. So Noah put out his hand and took the dove and brought it into the ark with him. He waited another seven days, and again he sent out the dove from the ark; and the dove came back to him in the evening, and there in its beak was a freshly plucked olive leaf; so Noah knew that the waters had subsided from the earth. Then he waited another seven days and sent out the dove; and it did not return to him any more.

In the six hundred first year, in the first month, the first day of the month, the waters were dried up from the earth; and Noah removed the covering of the ark, and looked, and saw that the face of the ground was drying. In the second month, on the twenty-seventh day of the month, the earth was dry. Then God said to Noah, "Go out of the ark, you and your wife, and your sons and your sons' wives with you. Bring out with you every living thing that is with you of all flesh — birds and animals and every creeping thing that creeps on the earth — so that they may abound on the earth, and be fruitful and multiply on the earth."

So Noah went out with his sons and his wife and his sons'

Genesis 8:6 – 18   wives.

DEATH had me in its grip,
the current swept me away;
Sheol was closing in,
I felt the hand of death.

From the depths I cried out,
my plea reached the heavens.
God heard me.

Then the earth shook:
the mountains quaked,
they rocked from side to side,
trembled at God's anger.

With fiery breath and blazing nostrils
God split open the heavens,
coming down on dense clouds,
riding on the cherubim throne,
soaring aloft with the winds.

Cloaked in darkness,
concealed in the rainstorm,
with flaming clouds,
with hail and coals of fire,
the Lord almighty
thundered from the heavens,
aimed lightning bolts like arrows
to rout the enemy.

At your rebuke, Lord,
when you bellowed in fury,
the bed of the ocean,
the foundations of the earth,
were laid bare.
From on high God took hold of me,
lifted me clear of the deadly waters.

God snatched me free,
led me to where I could breathe.
The Lord loved me.

Psalm 18:5 – 17, 20

GOD as the Bath: the primeval waters holding all earthly life before creation took form; the womb waters protecting and nurturing the preborn child; the dew with its nascent oxygen, cleaning dirty feet; soothing steam for aching limbs; a cold compress for fevered foreheads; tears to wash dust from the eyes. . . .

The people of God remember many divine baths. Naaman washes in the Jordan and is healed of leprosy. The blind man washes in Siloam's pool and receives his sight. But as the illustrator Peter Spier showed us, what about all the animals who were shut outside, watching Noah's ark as the water rose up their legs? The sea destroys the Egyptian army, and that sea, Leviathan's abode, is ready to drown Jonah. If God is the Bath, is God also the Flood, the waters from which we retreat and the waters within which we flounder?

Gail Ramshaw

EVEN as we live each day, death our life embraces.
Who is there to bring us help, rich, forgiving graces?
You only, Lord, you only!
Baptized in Christ's life-giving flood:
    water and his precious blood —

Holy and righteous God, Holy and mighty God,
Holy and all-merciful Savior,
Everlasting God, by grace bring us safely through the flood
    of bitter death. *Kyrieleis!*

Martin Luther
Sixteenth century

For a brief moment I abandoned you,
but with great compassion I will gather you.
In overflowing wrath for a moment
    I hid my face from you,
but with everlasting love I will have compassion on you,
    says the LORD, your Redeemer.

This is like the days of Noah to me:
    Just as I swore that the waters of Noah
    would never again go over the earth,
so I have sworn that I will not be angry with you
    and will not rebuke you.
For the mountains may depart
    and the hills be removed,
but my steadfast love shall not depart from you,
    and my covenant of peace shall not be removed,
    says the LORD, who has compassion on you.   Isaiah 54:7 – 10

God of the covenant,
as the forty days of deluge
swept away the world's corruption
and watered new beginnings
of righteousness and life,
so in the saving flood of baptism
we are washed clean and born again.

We beg you, unseal within us the wellspring of your grace,
cleanse our hearts of all that is not holy,
and cause your gift of new life to flourish once again.   Roman liturgy

THEN God said to Noah and to his sons with him, "As for me, I am establishing my covenant with you and your descendants after you, and with every living creature that is with you, the birds, the domestic animals and every animal of the earth with you, as many as came out of the ark. I establish my covenant with you, that never again shall all flesh be cut off by the waters of a flood, and never again shall there be a flood to destroy the earth." God said, "This is the sign of the covenant that I make between me and you and every living creature that is with you, for all future generations: I have set my bow in the clouds, and it shall be a sign of the covenant between me and the earth."

Genesis 9:8–13

WHEN we were lost
and could not find the way to you,
you loved us more than ever:
Jesus, your Son, innocent and without sin,
gave himself into our hands
and was nailed to a cross.
He stretched out his arms between heaven and earth
in the everlasting sign of your covenant.

Roman liturgy

WITH love I bow, with reverence bow before
my sacramental beginnings.
My darkness was always rain and turbulent waters,
a troubled world held in a crowded place.
My light was always rest on a mountaintop
in a new christened innocence of morning
with all the world washed clean.
The earth blushing with youth, dressed herself
in flowers and leaves,
and over all the sign of the sacred rainbow,
covenant like a poem one could read

over and over again and relish meaning,
itself arched doorway and a sudden entrance
to unexpected wisdom and delight.   Jessica Powers

A LL at once we find ourselves in a world of faith in
which rainfall and resurrection belong together. From
God's point of view the distinction between "natural" and
"supernatural," which has become so familiar to us, does
not exist. . . . The rain is no more natural than the resurrection and the resurrection no more miraculous than the rain.   Martin Buber

T HE little cloud increases still,
the heav'ns are big with rain;
We haste to catch the teeming show'r,
    and all its moisture drain.
A rill, a stream, a torrent flows,
    but pour the mighty flood;
O sweep the nations, shake the earth,
    'til all proclaim their God.

And when thou mak'st thy jewels up
    and set thy starry crown,
When all thy sparkling gems shall shine,
    proclaim'd by thee thine own,
May we, the little band of love,
    we sinners sav'd by grace,
From glory unto glory chang'd,   *Wyeth's Repository*
    behold thee face to face.   *of Sacred Music*

A BRAHAM rose early in the morning, saddled his donkey, and took two of his servants with him, and his son Isaac; he cut the wood for the burnt offering, and set out and went to the place in the distance that God had shown him. On the third day Abraham looked up and saw the place far away. Then Abraham said to his servants, "Stay here with the donkey; the boy and I will go over there; we will worship, and then we will come back to you." Abraham took the wood of the burnt offering and laid it on his son Isaac, and he himself carried the fire and the knife.

Genesis 22:3–6

W HY did Abraham accept in silence the command to sacrifice Isaac? Because he felt utter faith in God, was ready to give up all he owned and believed for the sake of his relationship with God? Or because he decided to test once and for all whether this God that he had followed was a murderer or not? Was Abraham a virtuoso of faith, or was he walking the knife-edge of despair?

Arthur I. Waskow

G OD of our ancestors:
What does it mean
that you so put a parent to the test,
to command Abraham to take the child's life,
even for you?
Are you not also a parent?
In this night's darkness
we want to know your beloved child Jesus,
who was bound Isaac-like to the wood of the cross
and so became the firstborn of the dead,
firstborn of those, countless as the stars,
among whom we would be counted.
Hear us, answer us,
for you are Lord for ever and ever.

Gabe Huck

Isaac said to his Father Abraham, "The fire and the wood are here, but where is the lamb for a burnt offering?" Abraham said, "It is God who will provide the lamb for a burnt offering, my son." So the two of them walked on together.

When they came to the place that God had shown him, Abraham built an altar there and laid the wood in order. He bound his son Isaac, and laid him on the altar, on top of the wood. Then Abraham reached out his hand and took the knife to kill his son.

Genesis 22:7–10

Such is the gift to you of this venerable Abraham, this patriarch, this noble respected chief, this abode of all virtues, this norm of sanctity, this perfection of priesthood! He offers today to the Lord in voluntary sacrifice his only son, the child of promise.

Gregory of Nazianzus
Fourth century

New ev'ry morning is the love
our waking and uprising prove;
through sleep and darkness safely brought,
restored to life, and pow'r, and thought.

If on our daily course our mind
be set to hallow all we find,
new treasures still of countless price
God will provide for sacrifice.

The trivial round, the common task
will furnish all we need or ask:
room to deny ourselves, a road
to bring us daily nearer God.

John Keble
Nineteenth century

ABRAHAM, patriarch beloved of God, who as a similitude of the Father didst offer thy son Isaac to him, for which thing in thee all the nations of the earth are blessed, mayest thou and may all the other patriarchs pray that I may daily offer my soul to Christ.

Saxon prayer
Eleventh century

THE angel of the LORD called from heaven, and said, "Abraham, Abraham!" And he said, "Here I am." The angel said, "Do not lay your hand on the boy or do anything to him; for now I know that you fear God, since you have not withheld your son, your only son, from me." And Abraham looked up and saw a ram, caught in a thicket by its horns. Abraham went and took the ram and offered it up as a burnt offering instead of his son.

Genesis 22:11 – 13

ABRAHAM sacrifices a ram as a substitute for Isaac. According to a tradition of the ancient rabbis, one horn of this ram became the shofar God blew at Mount Sinai to introduce the giving of the Ten Commandments, and the other horn will be used to announce the coming of Messiah.

Arthur I. Waskow

IN this church of God there is a large number of fathers listening to me. Do you think that any of you has acquired from the story of Abraham and Isaac such constancy, such strength of soul that if perchance your son were lost in death (which is universal and inescapable), even if he is your only son, beloved by you, would you think of the example of Abraham and place his magnanimity before your eyes?

Which of you thinks you will one day hear the voice of an angel saying: Now I know that you fear God because you did not spare your son, or your daughter, or husband, or wife, or you did not spare money, or earthly honors, or worldly ambitions, but you made light of everything and regarded everything as dung to gain Christ; you sold everything and gave to the poor, and followed the word of God? Which of you, do you think, will hear a statement like that?

Origen
Third century

E VER-FAITHFUL God,
with Abraham's obedience you were well pleased
and you accepted the sacrifice of your Son
who gave himself up for the sake of us all.

Train us by Christ's teaching
and school us in his obedience,
that as we walk his way of sacrifice,
we may come to share in his glory.

Roman liturgy

T HE angel of the LORD called to Abraham a second time from heaven, and said, "By myself I have sworn, says the LORD: Because you have done this, and have not withheld your son, your only son, I will indeed bless you, and I will make your offspring as numerous as the stars of heaven and as the sand that is on the seashore. And your offspring shall possess the gate of their enemies, and by your offspring shall all the nations of the earth gain blessing for themselves, because you have obeyed my voice."

Genesis 22:15 – 18

B LEST are you, Lord,
God of our ancestors,
worthy of praise
and renowned for ever.

Your works are true,
your ways straight,
your judgments sound,
your actions just.

For the sake of your good name,
do not abandon us,
do not break your oath.
Think of your beloved Abraham,
your servant Isaac, your holy Israel,
and do not withhold your love.

You promised them descendants
countless as the stars,
like sand on the shore.

Let a crushed heart and spirit
mean as much as countless offerings
of rams and sheep and bulls.
Let this be our sacrifice today,
let our loyalty win your favor,
for trust in you brings no shame.

Daniel 3:26–27,   Our hearts are completely yours.
34–36, 39–41   We fear yet seek your presence.

PROTECT me, God,
    I turn to you for help.
I profess, "You are my Lord,
my greatest good."

I once put faith in false gods,
the idols of the land.
Now I make no offering to them,
nor invoke their names.
Those who chase after them
add grief upon grief.

Lord, you measure out my portion,
the shape of my future;
you mark off the best place for me
to enjoy my inheritance.

I bless God who teaches me,
who schools my heart even at night.
I am sure God is here,
right beside me.
I cannot be shaken.

So my heart rejoices,
my body thrills with life,
my whole being rests secure.

You will not abandon me to Sheol,
nor send your faithful one to death.
You show me the road to life:
boundless joy at your side for ever!   Psalm 16

GOD and Father of all believers, for the glory of your
    name multiply, by the grace of the paschal sacrament,
the number of your children; that your church may rejoice   *Book of*
to see fulfilled your promise to our father Abraham.   *Common Prayer*

GOD and Father of all the faithful,
by the grace of adoption
you increase throughout the world the children
    of your promise;
in this paschal mystery you fulfill the pledge
made long ago to Abraham your servant,
that he would be father to many nations.
Grant that your people everywhere
may respond with faith to the grace of your calling.

Roman Missal

THEN the LORD said to Moses, "Why do you cry out to me? Tell the Israelites to go forward. But you lift up your staff, and stretch out your hand over the sea and divide it, that the Israelites may go into the sea on dry ground. Then I will harden the hearts of the Egyptians so that they will go in after them; and so I will gain glory for myself over Pharaoh and all his army, his chariots and his chariot drivers. And the Egyptians shall know that I am the LORD, when I have gained glory for myself over Pharaoh, his chariots and his chariot drivers."

The angel of God who was going before the Israelite army moved and went behind them; and the pillar of cloud moved from in front of them and took its place behind them. It came between the army of Egypt and the army of Israel. And so the cloud was there with the darkness, and it lit up the night; one did not come near the other all night.

Then Moses stretched out his hand over the sea. The LORD drove the sea back by a strong east wind all night and turned the sea into dry land, and the waters were divided. The Israelites went into the sea on dry ground, the waters forming a wall for them on their right and on their left. The Egyptians pursued and went into the sea after them, all of Pharaoh's horses, chariots and chariot drivers. At the morning watch the LORD in the pillar of fire and cloud looked down upon the Egyptian army and threw the Egyptian army into panic, clogging their chariot wheels so that they turned with difficulty. The Egyptians said, "Let us flee from the Israelites, for the LORD is fighting for them against Egypt."

Then the LORD said to Moses, "Stretch out your hand over the sea, so that the water may come back upon the Egyptians, upon their chariots and chariot drivers." So Moses stretched out his hand over the sea, and at dawn the sea returned to its normal depth. As the Egyptians fled before it, the LORD tossed the Egyptians into the sea. The waters returned and covered the chariots and the chariot drivers, the entire army of Pharaoh that had followed them into the sea; not one of them remained. But the Israelites walked on dry ground through the sea, the waters forming a wall for them on their right and on their left.

Thus the LORD saved Israel that day from the Egyptians, and Israel saw the Egyptians dead on the seashore. Israel saw the great work that the LORD did against the Egyptians. So the people feared the LORD and believed in the LORD and in Moses, the servant of the LORD. Exodus 14:15–30

THE high-tide of Easter drew nigh. Patrick thought that there was no place fitter for celebrating this chief solemnity of the year than in Mag Breg, in the place wherein was the chief abode of the idolatry and wizardry of Ireland, to wit, in Tara. Then he and his companions anchored their vessel in Inver Colptha and went along the land until they came to Ferta Fer Feicc [the Graves of Fiacc's Men], and Patrick's tent was pitched in that place, and he struck the paschal fire. It happened that that was the time at which was celebrated the high-tide of the heathen, to wit, the feast of Tara. The kings and the lords and the chiefs used to come to Tara, to Loegaire son of Niall, to celebrate the festival therein. The wizards, also, and the augurs would come so that they were prophesying to them. On that night, then, the fire of every hearth in Ireland was quenched, and it was proclaimed by the king that no fire should be kindled in Ireland before the fire of Tara. Patrick knew not that, and even though he had known, this would not have hindered him.

As the folk of Tara were biding there, they saw at some distance from them the paschal consecrated fire which Patrick had kindled. It lighted up the whole of Mag Breg. Then said the King: "That is a breach of a ban and law of mine. Find out who hath done so."

"We see," said the wizards, "the fire, and we know that unless it is quenched on the night on which it was made, it will not be quenched till doomsday. He, moreover, who kindles it will vanquish the kings and lords of Ireland unless he is forbidden."

Then the king was mightily disturbed. "This shall not be," saith he. "We will go and slay the man who kindled the fire." Then the chariots and his horses were yoked, and they went at the end of the night to the Graves of Fiacc's Men.

"Thou shouldst take heed," said the wizards, "not to go to the place where the fire was made, that thou mayst not do reverence to the man who kindled it, but stay outside and let him be called out to thee, that he may judge that thou art the king and that he is the subject, and we will argue in your presence."

They came thereafter and unyoked their horses and their chariots before the Graves. Patrick was called out to them after they had made a rule that no one should rise up to meet him lest he should believe in him. So Patrick arose and went forth, and saw the chariots and prophetic verse: "Some trust in chariots and some in horses, but we in the name of the Lord our mighty God." They were biding before him with the rims of their shields against their chins, and none rose up before him save one man only in whom was a nature from God, namely Erc son of Deg. Patrick bestowed a blessing upon him, and he believed in God and confessed the Catholic faith and was baptized.

The king, then, was greatly enraged against Patrick and wished at once to kill him. When Patrick saw the heathen arising against him, he cried with a great voice, and said: "Let God arise and let his enemies be scattered: Let them also that hate him flee before him. Like as the smoke vanished, so let them vanish; like as wax melteth at the fire, so let the ungodly perish at the presence of God." At once darkness came over the sun, and a great earthquake and trembling of arms took place there. It seemed to them that the sky fell on the earth, and the horses went off in fright, and the wind whirled the chariots through the fields.   *Life of St. Patrick*

M OSES, sing unto Christ thy King,
Who hath won the victory,
And hath laid low haughty Pharoah
Underneath the deep Red Sea.

God perforce overthrew the horse,
Rider, car and axle-tree.
They sank as lead, and their pow'r lie dead,
Dead as stone: so mote it be!

Your right hand and the wonder-wand
Did divide, at your decree,
The surging wave, and thereby did save
Us and ours from slavery.

Then merry, merry, merry, merry,
merry may we be,
As bird upon the berry
of the may or cherry tree,
as we stand with harp in hand
on the shore of the Red Sea.   *English carol*

A T that moment of the crossing, the ministering angels wanted to sing praises to God. But God silenced them, saying: "My children are drowning in the sea and you want to sing before me?"

Jewish midrash

G OD executed the judgment of death directly by God's selfsame power: "For I will go through the land of Egypt in that night. I and not any intermediary." Now obviously, the Holy One, blessed be God, could have given the children of Israel the power to avenge themselves upon the Egyptians, but God did not want to sanction the use of their fists for self-defense even at that time; for, while at that moment they might merely have defended themselves against evildoers, by such means the way of the fist spreads through the world, and in the end defenders become aggressors. Therefore, the Holy One, blessed be God, took great pains to remove Israel completely from any participation in the vengeance upon the evildoers, to such an extent that they were not permitted even to see the events.

The children of Israel, then, must derive this lesson from the events of that Passover eve: not to put their trust in wealth, and not to put their trust in might, but rather in the God of truth and justice, for this will serve to defend them everywhere against those who would dominate by the power of the fist.

Rabbi Aaron Samuel
Tamaret of Mileitchitz

W E have heard the story
our ancestors told us
of your deeds so long ago:

Sword did not win the land,
might did not bring the victory;
it was your power, your light,
your love for them.

Psalm 44:2, 4

THEN Moses and the Israelites
sang this song to the Lord:

I sing of the Lord,
great and triumphant:
horse and rider
are cast into the sea!

The Lord is my strength,
the Lord who saves me —
this is the God I praise,
the God of my ancestor.

True to the name "Lord,"
our God leads in battle,
hurls Pharaoh's chariots
and army into the sea.

The best of their warriors
sink beneath the Reed Sea,
sink like rocks to the bottom,
lie covered by the deep.

Your right arm, Lord,
is majesty and power,
your raised right arm
shatters the enemy.

Awesome your power:
you hurl down enemies,
you blaze forth in anger
to consume them like stubble.

One blast from your nostrils
and the waters pile high,
the waves pull back
to stand firm as a wall.

The enemy thinks, "Pursue them,
seize them and all they have,

feast on all their wealth,
draw the sword and destroy them."

But you send another blast;
the sea swallows them,
like lead they sink
in the terrifying waters.

Who can rival you, Lord,
among the gods?
Who can rival you,
terrifying in holiness?

Awesome this story,
fearful your wonders:
you stretched out your hand,
the earth swallowed them.

By your love you guide
this people you redeemed,
your power clears their path
to your holy place.

When nations hear, they shudder:
the Philistines writhe in fear,
all the princes of Edom
tremble in their terror,

all the chiefs of Moab
shake beyond control,
all the people of Canaan
melt away in dread.

Your mighty arm strikes terror,
they fall silent as stone,

while your people, Lord, cross over,
your own people cross over.

You brought and planted them, Lord,
on the mountain you chose,
where you make your dwelling,
the temple you built by hand.

The Lord rules for ever and ever!   Exodus 15:1 – 18

L IKE Moses in his song, we may now boast that Christ is
our praise and song and say with St. Paul that we should   Martin Luther
know nothing to sing or say save Jesus Christ our Savior.   Sixteenth century

T HIS is the night, God of Israel,
when first you saved our ancestors,
when the throng of Jacob's descendants,
leaving slavery behind,
saw the mighty waters of the sea turn back
so they could pass.
We who keep vigil here tonight
have met death in the waters of baptism,
and there we have put on life itself,
your child Jesus.   Gabe Huck

WHEN the road began to climb the first long swells of the Divide, Alexandra hummed an old Swedish hymn, and Emil wondered why his sister looked so happy. Her face was so radiant that he felt shy about asking her. For the first time, perhaps, since that land emerged from the waters of geologic ages, a human face was set toward it with love and yearning. It seemed beautiful to her, rich and strong and glorious. Her eyes drank in the breadth of it, until her tears blinded her. Then the genius of the Divine, the great, free spirit which breathes across it, must have bent lower than it ever bent to a human will before.

Willa Cather

NOT only our ancestors alone did the Holy One redeem but us as well, along with them, as it is written: "And God freed us from Egypt so as to take us and give us the land which the LORD had sworn to our ancestors."

A Passover Haggadah

I waited and waited for God.
At long last God bent down
to hear my complaint,
and pulled me from the grave
out of the swamp,
and gave me a steady stride
on rock-solid ground.

God taught me a new song,
a hymn of praise.
Seeing all this,
many will be moved
to trust in the Lord.

I celebrate your justice
before all the assembly;
I do not hold back the story.
Lord, you know this is true.

Psalm 40:2–4, 10

O NLY that great moment when they set me free
From barbed-wire fences and the lightless prisons,
That moment suddenly arrived, unguarded,
With early March's glittering frost, and heaven
Lit up with stars at noon, and on my lips
The blessing not said since childhood suddenly
Recalled as if it were but yesterday —
I make myself believe: to every lover
of humankind that day will be a holiday,
Arriving without asking to come in.   Samuel Halkin

L ORD God,
in the new covenant
you shed light on the miracles you worked
   in ancient times:
the Red Sea is a symbol of our baptism,
and the nation you freed from slavery
is a sign of your Christian people.
May every nation
share the faith and privilege of Israel
and come to new birth in the Holy Spirit.   *Roman Missal*

T HEN the prophet Miriam took a tambourine in her hand;
and all the women went out after her with tambourines
and with dancing. And Miriam sang to them:

   "Sing to the Lord,
   for he has triumphed gloriously;
   horse and rider he has thrown into the sea."   Exodus 15:20–21

THE Israelites, when they got free,
From the Pharaoh's land, in haste did flee,
And on the banks of the Red Sea,
A joyful scene commenced;
An Elder sister led the band,
With sounding timbrel in her hand,
While virgins moved by her command,
And after her they danced.

Shaker song
Nineteenth century

SHAKE tambourines! Clash cymbals!
Strike up a song to my God!
Sound a new music of praise!
Praise and call on God's name!

I sing my God a fresh new song:
"Grandeur and glory are yours, Lord,
with power that astonishes all;
no rival can match your might.

"Let all creation bend to you:
for you spoke, and they took shape;
you breathed, they came alive.
No one can resist your voice.

"Mountain peak and ocean depth
quake to their inmost core.
Rocks melt like wax when you appear —
while you spare those who stand in awe."

Judith 16:1, 13 – 15

THE one who once
hid the pursuing tyrant
in the waves of the sea,
was hidden beneath the earth. . . .
But let us, as the maidens,
Sing unto the Lord,
For God is greatly glorified.

Kassia
Ninth century

IT is possible for there to be possibility.

In Exodus, the women keep on teaching the lesson. Pharaoh's daughter and Miriam conspire to save the life of a baby boy by giving him a second birth from the water of the Nile — and he grows up to be Moses. But even Moses must receive more education from women before he can become the liberator. His first clumsy efforts at liberation only send him bursting forth from Egypt like tumultuously sown seed. He settles among seven women at a well (a symbol of the womb), marries one of them, has a child — and *only then* can meet God at the burning bush and hear the Voice and Name of freedom. Even this is not enough: on the journey back to Egypt, Moses — in danger of death — has to learn from his wife Tzipporah how to fulfill the birth of his son by renewing the covenant of circumcision. Not till then can he take on the task he has been assigned.

Women — and the quintessentially female process, giving birth to children — were crucial to the liberation from Egypt. Even the liberation itself — out of *mitzrayim* (Egypt), the "tight spot," across the broken waters of the Red Sea — was a birth, or a conception in the first stages of what became a birth on crossing Jordan. Torah shows us that the process cannot be fulfilled until men are also part of it. But it is the women who first understand the path.

Arthur I. Waskow

Let me share a story I heard in Kenya: The 30 small Christian communities in the parish of Thika outside Nairobi prepare all year for the Easter Vigil, which lasts from 7:00 PM until 7:00 AM. One of the small communities proclaimed the Exodus reading. Then a *yangyangtiti* (a kind of town crier) sang of oppression and slavery in their own community. Such singing often lands people in jail.

The entire assembly then marched through strands of blue crepe paper (their Red Sea) and sang Miriam's song of praise and freedom. After the Vigil, one small community continued to vigil and to march for freedom by going to a plant that was spewing toxic waste into the air and water. They demonstrated for its closure and were jailed.

James B. Dunning

God of our ancestors,
even in these present days
the wonders of your ancient deeds shine forth:
your right hand parted the waters
and delivered a single people from the slavery of Pharaoh;
now through the waters of rebirth
you extend to every nation
deliverance from the bondage of sin.
Grant that all the peoples of the world
may become children of Abraham
and enter the inheritance promised to Israel.

Roman Missal

For your Maker is your husband,
the Lord of hosts is his name;
the Holy One of Israel is your Redeemer,
    the God of the whole earth he is called.

For the LORD has called you
    like a wife forsaken and grieved in spirit,
like the wife of a man's youth when she is cast off,
    says your God.
For a brief moment I abandoned you,
    but with great compassion I will gather you.
In overflowing wrath for a moment
    I hid my face from you,
but with everlasting love I will have compassion on you,
    says the LORD, your Redeemer.

This is like the days of Noah to me:
    Just as I swore that the waters of Noah
    would never again go over the earth,
so I have sworn that I will not be angry with you
    and will not rebuke you.
For the mountains may depart
    and the hills be removed,
but my steadfast love shall not depart from you,
    and my covenant of peace shall not be removed,
    says the LORD, who has compassion on you.

O afflicted one, storm-tossed, and not comforted,
    I am about to set your stones in antimony,
    and lay your foundations with sapphires.
I will make your pinnacles of rubies,
    your gates of jewels,
    and all your wall of precious stones.

All your children shall be taught by the LORD,
    and great shall be the prosperity of your children.
In righteousness you shall be established;
    you shall be far from oppression, for you shall not fear;
    and from terror, for it shall not
        come near you.

                                            Isaiah 54:5–14

I give you high praise,
for you, Lord, raised me up
above my gloating enemy.
Lord, how I begged you,
and you, God, healed me.
You pulled me from the pit,
brought me back from Sheol.

Celebrate, all you saints,
praise this awesome God,
Whose anger passes quickly,
whose mercy lasts a lifetime —
as laughter fills a day
after one brief night of tears.

When all was going well,
I thought I could never fall;
with God's powerful blessing,
I would stand like a mountain!
Then you hid your face;
I shook with fear!

I cried out, "Lord, Lord!"
I begged, I pleaded:
"What good is my blood to you?
Why push me down the pit?
Can dead bones praise you,
recount your unbroken love?
Listen to me, O God,
turn and help me now."

You changed my anguish
into this joyful dance,
pulled off my sackcloth,
gave me bright new robes,
that my life might sing your glory,
never silent in your praise.
For ever I will thank you,
Psalm 30   O Lord my God.

ALMIGHTY and eternal God,
for the glory of your name
fulfill the promise you made long ago
to men and women of faith,
to bless them with descendants for ever.
Increase your adopted children throughout the world,
that your church may see accomplished
the salvation which those saints of old so firmly expected.   *Roman Missal*

HO, everyone who thirsts,
come to the waters;
and you that have no money,
    come, buy and eat!
Come, buy wine and milk
    without money and without price.
Why do you spend your money for that which is not bread,
    and your labor for that which does not satisfy?
Listen carefully to me, and eat what is good,
    and delight yourselves in rich food.

Incline your ear, and come to me;
    listen, so that you may live.
I will make with you an everlasting covenant,
    my steadfast, sure love for David.
See, I made him a witness to the peoples,
    a leader and commander for the peoples.
See, you shall call nations that you do not know,

and nations that do not know you shall run to you,
because of the LORD your God, the Holy One of Israel.
for the LORD has glorified you.

Seek the LORD while the LORD may be found,
call upon God while God is near;
let the wicked forsake their way,
and the unrighteous their thoughts;
let them return to the LORD, who will have mercy on them,
and to our God, who will abundantly pardon.
For my thoughts are not your thoughts,
nor are your ways my ways, says the LORD.
For as the heavens are higher than the earth,
so are my ways higher than your ways
and my thoughts than your thoughts.

For as the rain and the snow come down from heaven,
and do not return there until they have watered the earth,
making it bring forth and sprout,
giving seed to the sower and bread to the eater,
so shall my word be that goes out from my mouth;
it shall not return to me empty,
but it shall accomplish that which I purpose,
and succeed in the thing for
Isaiah 55:1 – 11   which I sent it.

I praise you, Lord!
When your rage turned on me,
you turned it away
and now you console me.

God is my savior,
my trust knows no fear;
God's strength is my strength,
yes, God is my savior.

With joy you will draw water
from God's saving well;
then you will say to each other,
"Praise the Lord! proclaim God's name!"

Tell the world what God does,
make known this magestic name.
Sing the wonders God works,
recount them in every land.

Shout and sing for joy,
citizens of Zion,
for great among you
is the Holy One of Israel!   Isaiah 12:1–6

ALMIGHTY and eternal God,
only true hope of the world,
through the voices of your prophets
you announced the mysteries we celebrate tonight.
Stir up the longings of your faithful people,
because we grow in holiness
only through the prompting of your grace.   *Roman Missal*

Hear the commandments of life,
  O Israel;
    give ear, and learn wisdom!
Why is it, O Israel, why is it that you are in the land of
      your enemies,
    that you are growing old in a foreign country,
that you are defiled with the dead,
    that you are counted among those in Hades?
You have forsaken the fountain of wisdom.
If you had walked in the way of God,
  you would be living in peace forever.
Learn where there is wisdom,
  where there is strength,
  where there is understanding,
so that you may at the same time discern
  where there is length of days, and life,
  where there is light for the eyes, and peace.

Who has found the place of Wisdom?
  And who has entered her storehouses?

But the one who knows all things knows her,
  and found her through understanding.
The one who prepared the earth for all time
filled it with four-footed creatures;
the one who sends forth the light, and it goes;
  called it, and it hearkened, trembling;
the stars shone in their watches, and were glad;
  God called them, and they said, "Here we are!"
  They shone with gladness for the one who made them.
This is our God,
  to whom no other can be compared.
God found the whole way to knowledge,

and gave her to Jacob, God's servant, Jacob
and to Israel, the one whom God loved.
Afterward she appeared on earth
and lived with humankind.

She is the book of the commandments of God,
the law that endures forever.
All who hold her fast will live,
and those who forsake her will die.

Turn, O Jacob, and take her;
walk toward the shining of her light.
Do not give your glory to another,
or your advantages to an alien people.
Happy are we, O Israel,
for we know what is pleasing to God.

Baruch 3:9 – 15, 32;
4:1 – 4

G OD's perfect law
revives the soul.
God's stable rule
guides the simple.

God's just demands
delight the heart,
God's clear commands
sharpen vision.

God's faultless decrees
stand for ever.
God's right judgments
keep their truth.

Their worth is more than gold,
the purest gold;
their taste richer than honey,
sweet from the comb.

Psalm 19:8 – 11

Now all the heav'nly splendor
Breaks forth in starlight tender
From myriad worlds unknown;
And we, this marvel seeing,
Forget our selfish being
For joy of beauty not our own.

Though long our ancient blindness
Has missed God's loving kindness
And plunged us into strife;
One day, when life is over,
Shall death's fair night uncover
The fields of everlasting life.

Paul Gerhardt
Seventeenth century

God of life,
by calling all nations to be saved
you cause your Church to grow.
In your mercy hear our prayers
and keep forever safe
those whom you cleanse in the waters of baptism.

Roman Missal

The word of the LORD came to me: Mortal, when the house of Israel lived in their own soil, they defiled it with their ways and their deeds; so I poured out my wrath upon them for the blood that they had shed upon the land, and for the idols with which they had defiled it. I scattered them among the nations, and they were dispersed through the countries; in accordance with their conduct and their deeds I judged them. But when they came to the nations, wherever they came, they profaned my holy name, in that it was said of them. "These are the people of the LORD, and yet they had to go out of his land." But I had concern for my holy name, which the house of Israel had proclaimed among the nations to which they came.

Therefore say to the house of Israel, Thus says the LORD GOD: It is not for your sake, O house of Israel, that I am about to act, but for the sake of my holy name, which you have profaned among the nations to which you came. I will sanctify my great name, which has been profaned among the nations, and which you have profaned among them; and the nations shall know that I am the LORD, says the LORD GOD, when through you I display my holiness before their eyes. I will take you from the nations, and gather you from all the countries, and bring you into your own land. I will sprinkle clean water upon you, and you shall be clean from all your uncleannesses, and from all your idols I will cleanse you. A new heart I will give you, and a new spirit I will put within you; and I will remove from your body the heart of stone and give you a heart of flesh. I will put my spirit within you, and make you follow my statutes and be careful to observe my ordinances. Then you shall live in the land that I gave to your ancestors; and you shall be my people, and I will be your God.

Ezekiel 36:16 – 28

CREATOR, reshape my heart,
God, steady my spirit.
Do not cast me aside
stripped of your holy spirit.

Save me, bring back my joy,
support me, strengthen my will.
Then I will teach your way
and sinners will turn to you.

When I offer a holocaust,
the gift does not please you.
So I offer my shattered spirit;
a changed heart you welcome.

Psalm 51:12 – 15,
18 – 19

I thirst for God,
the living God.
When will I see your face?

I cry my heart out,
I remember better days:
when I entered the house of God,
I was caught in the joyful sound
of pilgrims giving thanks.

Send your light and truth.
They will escort me
to the holy mountain
where you make your home.

I will approach the altar of God,
God, my highest joy,
and praise you with the harp,
God, my God.

Psalm 42:3, 5
Psalm 43:3 – 4

WITH all our hearts, even our hearts of stone,
we ask you, Lord, that we might come this night
to the long-promised land, the land of milk and honey,
the land where your name is made holy in deeds of justice,
the hungry fed and the naked clothed,
prisoners set free, creation reverenced,
and all to share and share alike at your table.

Gabe Huck

Gᴏᴅ of power and unwavering light,
look with mercy on your great sacrament, the church,
and bring to fulfillment
your eternal plan of redemption.
Then may the whole world see and know
that the fallen has been raised again,
the old has been shaped anew,
and that all has been restored to wholeness
through Christ himself,
the beginning and end of all things.
Roman Missal

Lᴏʀᴅ God,
in both Testaments of Holy Scripture,
you teach us to celebrate the paschal mystery.
Grant that we may understand the workings of your mercy,
so that the gifts we receive today
may confirm our hope of blessings to come.
Roman Missal

Tʜᴇ hand of the Lᴏʀᴅ came upon me, and he brought me out by the spirit of the Lᴏʀᴅ and set me down in the middle of a valley; it was full of bones. The Lᴏʀᴅ led me all around them; there were very many lying in the valley, and they were very dry. The Lᴏʀᴅ said to me, "Mortal, can these bones live?" I answered, "O Lord Gᴏᴅ, you know." Then the Lᴏʀᴅ said to me, "Prophesy to these bones, and say to them: O dry bones, hear the word of the Lᴏʀᴅ. Thus says the Lord Gᴏᴅ to these bones: I will cause breath to enter you, and you shall live. I will lay sinews on you, and will cause flesh to come upon you and cover you with skin, and put breath in you, and you shall live; and you shall know that I am the Lᴏʀᴅ."

So I prophesied as I had been commanded; and as I prophesied, suddenly there was a noise, a rattling, and the bones came together, bone to its bone. I looked, and there were sinews on them, and flesh had come upon them, and skin had covered them; but there was no breath in them. Then the LORD said to me, "Prophesy to the breath, prophesy, mortal, and say to the breath, Thus says the Lord GOD: Come from the four winds, O breath, and breathe upon these slain, that they may live." I prophesied as he commanded me, and the breath came into them, and they lived, and stood on their feet, a vast multitude.

Then the LORD said to me, "Mortal, these bones are the whole house of Israel. They say, 'Our bones are dried up, and our hope is lost; we are cut off completely.' Therefore prophesy, and say to them, Thus says the Lord GOD: I am going to open your graves and bring you up from your graves, O my people; and I will bring you back to the land of Israel. And you shall know that I am the LORD, when I open your graves and bring you up from your graves, O my people. I will put my spirit within you, and you shall live, and I will place you on your own soil; then you shall know that I, the LORD, have spoken and will act," says the LORD.

Ezekiel 37:1–14

H EAR me, faithful Lord!
bend to my prayer,
show compassion.
Do not judge me harshly:
in your sight, no one is just.

My enemy hunts me down,
grinding me to dust,
caging me with the dead
in lasting darkness.
My strength drains away,
my heart is numb.

I remember the ancient days,
I recall your wonders,
the work of your hands.
Dry as thirsty land,
I reach out for you.

Answer me quickly, Lord.
my strength is spent.
Do not hide from me
or I will fall into the grave.

Let morning announce your love,
for it is you I trust.
Show me the right way,
I offer you myself.

Rescue me from my foes,
you are my only refuge, Lord.
Teach me your will,
for you are my God.

Graciously lead me, Lord,
on to level ground.
I call on your just name,
keep me safe, free from danger.

In your great love for me,
disarm my enemies,
destroy their power,
for I belong to you.   Psalm 143

O God, by the Passover of the Son
you have brought us out of sin into righteousness
and out of death into life.
Grant to those who are sealed by your Holy Spirit   *Book of*
the will and power to proclaim you to all the world.   *Alternative Services*

Sing aloud, O daughter Zion;
shout, O Israel!
Rejoice and exult with all your heart,
O daughter Jerusalem!

The LORD has taken away the judgments against you,
and has turned away your enemies.
The Sovereign of Israel, the LORD, is in your midst;
you shall fear disaster no more.

On that day it shall be said to Jerusalem:
Do not fear, O Zion;
do not let your hands grow weak.

The LORD, your God, is in your midst,
a warrior who gives victory;
the LORD will rejoice over you with gladness,
and renew you with love;
the LORD will exult over you with loud singing
as on a day of festival.
I will remove disaster from you,
so that you will not bear reproach for it.

I will deal with all your oppressors at that time.
And I will save the lame
and gather the outcast,
and I will change their shame into praise
and renown in all the earth.

At that time I will bring you home,
at the time when I gather you;
for I will make you renowned and praised
among all the peoples of the earth,
when I restore your fortunes
Zephaniah 3:14–20   before your eyes, says the LORD.

O God of unchangeable power and eternal light: Look favorably on your whole church, that wonderful and sacred mystery; by the effectual working of your providence, carry out in tranquillity the plan of salvation; let the whole world see and know that things which were cast down are being raised up, and things which had grown old are being made new, and that all things are being brought to their perfection by him through whom all things are made, your Son Jesus Christ our Lord.   *Book of Common Prayer*

O N that day the branch of the Lord shall be beautiful and glorious, and the fruit of the land shall be the pride and glory of the survivors of Israel. Whoever is left in Zion and remains in Jerusalem will be called holy, everyone who has been recorded for life in Jerusalem, once the Lord has cleansed the bloodstains of Jerusalem from its midst by a spirit of judgment and by a spirit of burning. Then the Lord will create over the whole site of Mount Zion and over its places of assembly a cloud by day and smoke and the shining of a flaming fire by night. Indeed over all the glory there will be a canopy. It will serve as a pavilion, a shade by day from the heat, and a refuge and a shelter from the storm and rain.   Isaiah 4:2–6

L ET me sing for my beloved
my love-song concerning my beloved's vineyard:
"My beloved had a vineyard on a very fertile hill.
My beloved dug it and cleared it of stones,
and planted it with choice vines;
built a watchtower in the midst of it,
and hewed out a wine vat in it."

For the vineyard of the Lord of hosts is the house of Israel,
and the people of Judah are God's pleasant planting.   Isaiah 5:1–2, 7

Lutheran Book of Worship

O God, by the word of the prophets you are known in the church as the sower of the good seed, the keeper of the chosen vineyard. Grant to your people who are called your vine and your harvest, that, cleansed of all thorns and briars, they may abundantly bring forth good fruit.

Jonah 3:5 – 9

THE people of Nineveh believed God; they proclaimed a fast, and everyone, great and small, put on sackcloth.

When the news reached the king of Nineveh, he rose from his throne, removed his robe, covered himself with sackcloth and sat in ashes. Then he had a proclamation made in Nineveh: "By the decree of the king and his nobles: No human being or animal, no herd or flock, shall taste anything. They shall not feed, nor shall they drink water. Human beings and animals shall be covered with sackcloth, and they shall cry mightily to God. All shall turn from their evil ways and from the violence that is in their hands. Who knows? God may relent so that we do not perish."

Lutheran Book of Worship

O God, you have united all nations in the confession of your name. Now give us the will and the power to do what you command, that the faith of the people whom you call to everlasting life may direct their speech and actions.

Now therefore write this song, and teach it to the Israelites; put it in their mouths, in order that this song may be a witness for me against the Israelites. For when I have brought them into the land flowing with milk and honey, which I promised on oath to their ancestors, and they have eaten their fill and grown fat, they will turn to other gods and serve them, despising me and breaking my covenant. And when many terrible troubles come upon them, this song will confront them as a witness, because it will not be lost from the mouths of their descendants. For I know what they are inclined to do even now, before I have brought them into the land that I promised them on oath." That very day Moses wrote this song and taught it to the Israelites.

Deuteronomy
31:19–22

Give ear to what I say, you heavens,
and let the earth hear the words of my mouth.

My teaching shall fall like drops of rain;
my words shall distill as the dew,

Like fine rain upon the grass
and like the showers on young plants.

When I call aloud in the name of the LORD,
you shall respond, "Great is our God,

the rock whose work is perfect,
and all his ways are just;

a faithful God, who does no wrong,
righteous and true is he."

Remember the days of old;
think of the generations long ago;

ask your father to recount it
and your elders to tell you the tale.

The LORD will give his people justice
and have compassion on his servants.

Deuteronomy 32:1–4,
7, 36, 43

Rejoice with him, you heavens;
all you gods, bow down before him.

O God, exaltation of the humble and strength of the righteous: You taught your people through Moses to sing your praise, that the law which he delivered to them might be helpful to us. Show your power among all nations that, in the forgiveness of sins, terror may turn to joy, and fear of retribution to salvation.

Lutheran Book
of Worship

Daniel 6:16–18

THE king gave the command, and Daniel was brought and thrown into the den of lions. The king said to Daniel, "May your God, whom you faithfully serve, deliver you!" A stone was brought and laid on the mouth of the den, and the king sealed it with his own signet and with the signet of his lords, so that nothing might be changed concerning Daniel. Then the king went to his palace and spent the night fasting; no food was brought to him, and sleep fled from him.

DANIEL faithful to his God
would not bow down to men,
And by God's enemy he was hurled
   into a lion's den.
God locked the lions' jaws we read
   and robbed them of their prey.
And the God that lived in Daniel's time
   is just the same today.

   Is just the same today!
   Just the same today!
   The God that lived in Daniel's time
   Is just the same today!

African American
spiritual

TURN to God, be bright with joy;
you shall never be let down.
I begged and God heard,
took my burdens from me.

God's angel defends the faithful,
guards them on every side.
Drink in the richness of God,
enjoy the strength of the Lord.

Live in awe of God, you saints:
you will want for nothing.
Even if lions go hungry,
those seeking God are fed.

Psalm 34:6 – 11

NEBUCHADNEZZAR was so filled with rage against Shadrach, Meshach and Abednego that his face was distorted. He ordered the furnace heated up seven times more than was customary and ordered some of the strongest guards in his army to bind Shadrach, Meshach and Abednego and to throw them into the furnace of blazing fire. So the men were bound, still wearing their tunics, their trousers, their hats and their other garments, and they were thrown into the furnace of blazing fire.

Daniel 3:19–21

Do not fear, the fire will do you no harm,
For it will have strength against your enemies.
I have given orders that it fast as you do
And that it greedily devour the greedy
   who do not sing with you.

Romanos
Sixth century

KING Nebuchadnezzar was astonished and said to his counselors, "Was it not three men that we threw bound into the fire?" They answered the king, "True, O king." He replied, "But I see four men unbound, walking in the middle of the fire, and they are not hurt; and the fourth has the appearance of a god." Nebuchadnezzar then approached the door of the furnace of blazing fire and said, "Shadrach, Meshach and Abednego, servants of the Most High God, come out!"

Daniel 3:24–26

WHERE are the Hebrew children?
Where are the Hebrew children?
Where are the Hebrew children?
   Safe in the promised land!
Though the furnace flamed around them,
God while in their trouble found them,

God with love and mercy bound them
    Safe in the promised land!

By and by we'll go and meet them,
By and by we'll go and meet them,
By and by we'll go and meet them,
    Safe in the promised land!
There our souls will join the chorus,
Saints and angels, sing before us,
While all heav'n is beaming o'er us,
    Safe in the promised land!

African American
spiritual

CHRIST rises from the grave, Christ who freed the three
children from the forge of burning fire.

Monastic antiphonal

THE power of the furnace was instantly destroyed,
    For an angel suddenly descended from heaven,
Moved into the middle of the furnace, and completely
        appeased the fire
    And made it into a paradise for the holy youths.
They walked on the coals as though they were roses,
    And they luxuriated in the sparks as though
        they were flowers.
The place that was a crematorium became an oratory;
    It seemed like a rose-strewn inner chamber.
The furnace, which breathed death to those near and far,
    Did not disturb the life of those in its midst, for it feared
        what they sang.

Romanos
Sixth century

Wouldst thou know my meaning?
Lie down in the fire.
See and ask the flowing
Godhead through thy being;
Feel the Holy Spirit
Moving and compelling
Thee within the glowing
Fire and light of God.

Mechthilde
of Magdeburg
Thirteenth century

Blest are you, God of our ancestors,
praised and lifted above all for ever!
Blest your holy name, full of wonder,
praised and lifted above all for ever!

Blest are you in your temple of glory,
acclaimed and honored for ever!
Blest are you who see the depths
from the cherubim throne,
praised and lifted above all for ever!

Blest are you enthroned in majesty,
praised and lifted above all for ever!
Blest are you beyond the stars,
acclaimed and honored for ever!
All you creatures, bless our God,
acclaimed and exalted for ever!

Daniel 3:52–57

O ye angels of the Lord, bless ye the Lord,
praise and magnify the Lord for ever.
O ye Saints of the Isles, bless ye the Lord.
O ye Servants of Christ who here sang
   God's praises and thence went forth
   to preach, bless ye the Lord.
O ye souls of the faithful, who rest in Jesus,
O ye kindly folk of the Island,
O ye pilgrims who seek joy and health
   in this beloved Isle, bless ye the Lord.

O ye sheep and horned cattle,
O ye lambs that gambol on the sward,
O ye seals that glisten in the waters,
    bless ye the Lord.
O ye ravens and hoodies,
O ye rooks that caw from the sycamores,
O ye buzzards that float on the
    wind-currents, bless ye the Lord.
O ye gulls that fill the beaches with
    your clamour,
O ye terns and gannets that dive
    headlong for your prey
O ye curlews and landrails,
O ye pied shelduck and Bride's ghillies,
O ye dunlins that wheel in unison over
    the waves, bless ye the Lord.
O ye larks that carol in the heavens,
O ye blackbirds that pipe at the dawning,
O ye pipits and wheatears,
O ye warblers and wrens that make
    the glens joyful with song,
O ye bees that love the heather,
    bless ye the Lord.
O ye primroses and bluebells,
O ye flowerets that gem the marsh with colour
O ye golden flags that deck Columba's
    Bay with glory, bless ye the Lord.
O ye piled rocks fashioned by Nature's
    might thro' myriad ages.
O ye majestic Bens of Mull,
O ye white sands and emerald shallows
O ye blue and purple deeps of ocean,
O ye winds and clouds, bless ye the Lord.
O all ye works of the Lord, bless ye the
    Lord, praise and magnify the Lord
    for ever.

An Iona *Benedicite*
E. D. Sedding

A FTER the last reading from the Old Testament with its responsory and prayer, the altar candles may be lighted, and the Gloria is sung by all present. The church bells may be rung, according to local custom.

Roman Missal

I N addition to calling the assembly, bells have been used to draw those absent from the assembly into prayerful union; for example, during high moments of the eucharistic prayer or during special hymns of praise. Through the Middle Ages, they also were utilized as civic clocks, as invitations to non-liturgical private prayer (the times of the Angelus prayer) and as heralds of extraordinary events.

G. Thomas Ryan

I will sing a Gloria that shall fill the top of my towers
     with the clangour of their bells.
Praise the Lord all sorrow of the earth!
Let the impoverished praise him, and those who are in exile,
     let the disappointed praise him, and the disinherited,
     let him be praised by all whom nothing satisfies.
Be he praised by the bright torment of the spirit, and by
     the dark torment of nature.
Be he praised by the holy torment of love.
Be he praised by the solitude of the soul and
     by the soul's captivity.
Be he praised by the sorrow of sin and by the woe that
     all things perish
Be he praised also by the bitter anguish of death.
For the sorrow of the world has become blessed, because it
     has been loved.
Behold the wood of the Cross on which hung the
     salvation of the world.

Gertrude von Le Fort

O God,
your saving plan has brought us
to the glory of this night.
Slaves, we become your sons and daughters,
poor, your mercy makes us rich,
sinners, you count us among your saints.
Bring us to know the place that is ours
in the unfolding story of your purpose,
and instill in our hearts
the wonder of your salvation.

Roman Missal

ETERNAL Giver of life and light,
this holy night shines with the radiance
    of the risen Christ.
Renew your church with the Spirit given to us in baptism,
that we may worship you in sincerity and truth,
and shine as a light in the world.

*Book of
Common Worship*

GRACIOUS God,
you have made us one
with all your people in heaven and on earth.
We have recalled your mighty acts in holy history.
We have seen your power
in sending light to conquer darkness,
water to give us life;
and the bread of heaven to nourish us in love.
Send us with your salvation and joy to all the world,
in the name of Jesus Christ our Lord.

*Book of
Common Worship*

D o you not know that all of us who have been baptized into Christ Jesus were baptized into his death? Therefore we have been buried with Christ by baptism into death, so that, just as Christ was raised from the dead by the glory of the Father, so we too might walk in newness of life.

For if we have been united with Christ in a death like his, we will certainly be united with him in a resurrection like his.

We know that our old self was crucified with Christ so that the body of sin might be destroyed and we might no longer be enslaved to sin. For whoever has died is freed from sin. But if we have died with Christ, we believe that we will also live with him. We know that Christ, being raised from the dead, will never die again; death no longer has dominion over him. The death he died, he died to sin, once for all; but the life he lives, he lives to God. So you also must consider

Romans 6:3 – 11   yourselves dead to sin and alive to God in Christ Jesus.

T HROUGH Jesus' suffering and exaltation all other sufferers are now healed. All other sufferers may now join in the thanksgiving hymn of Psalm 118. Through him God has answered us all. . . . God's Son, the cornerstone, has been exalted by God and it is wonderful in our eyes. But that is not enough for God's enduring love. We hope for exaltation too. Our hope stretches toward a future when even we shall

Irene Nowell   be like God.

G IVE thanks, the Lord is good,
God's love is for ever!
Now let Israel say,
"God's love is for ever!"

Let the house of Aaron say,
"God's love is for ever!"
Let all who revere the Lord say,
"God's love is for ever!"

In distress I called to the Lord,
who answered and set me free.
The Lord is with me, I fear not.
What can they do to me?
The Lord my help is with me,
I can face my foes.

I was pushed to falling,
but the Lord gave me help.
My strength, my song is the Lord,
who has become my savior.

Glad songs of victory sound
within the tents of the just.
With right hand raised high,
the Lord strikes with force.

I shall not die but live
to tell the Lord's great deeds.
The Lord punished me severely,
But did not let me die.

Open the gates of justice,
let me praise God within them.
This is the Lord's own gate,
only the just will enter.
I thank you for you answered me,
and you became my savior.

The stone the builders rejected
has become the cornerstone.

This is the work of the Lord,
how wonderful in our eyes.

This is the day the Lord made,
let us rejoice and be glad.
Lord, give us the victory!
Lord, grant us success!

Blest is the one who comes,
who comes in the name of the Lord.
We bless you from the Lord's house.
The Lord God is our light:
adorn the altar with branches.

I will thank you, my God,
I will praise you highly.

Psalm 118:1 – 7,
13 – 29

Give thanks, the Lord is good,
God's love is for ever!

Ceremonial of Bishops

One of the deacons goes to the bishop and says to him:

MOST Reverend Father, I bring you a message of great
joy, the message of Alleluia.

Liber Usualis

A L-le-   lú-   ia.

L ᴇᴛ us chant Alleluia. Then the word of scripture will be accomplished, the word not of combatants any more, but of victors; *Death has been swallowed up in victory!*

Let us chant Alleluia. *O Death, where is your sting?*

Let us chant Alleluia. *The sting of death is sin* (1 Corinthians 15:56). *You will seek its place and will not find it* (Psalm 37:10).

Let us chant Alleluia here in the midst of dangers and temptations, we and the others. *God is faithful,* says the apostle, *he will not allow us to be tempted above our ability* (1 Corinthians 10:13).

O blessed Alleluia of heaven! No more anguish, no more adversity. No more enemy. No more love of destruction. Up above, praise to God, and here below, praise to God. Praise mingled with fear here, but without disturbance above. Here we chant in hope, there, in possession; here it is Alleluia *en route,* there it is Alleluia on arriving home.

Augustine
Fifth century

A ʟʟᴇʟᴜɪᴀ is interpreted as "Praise God." To be sure, that is a short word, but it is a great praise.

Caesarius of Arles
Sixth century

T ʜᴇ Alleluia is not for what was; Easter proclaims a beginning which has already decided the remotest future. The resurrection means that the beginning of glory has already started. And what began in that way is in process of fulfillment.

And so we comprise the whole history of nature and of humankind in a celebration which in rite contains the actual reality celebrated, and we make the ultimate statement about it: I believe in the resurrection of the body and life everlasting. I believe that the beginning of the glory of all things has already come upon us, that we, apparently so lost, wandering and seeking far away, are already encompassed by infinite blessedness. For the end has already begun. And it is glory.

Karl Rahner

Gerard S. Sloyan

So sing Alleluia whether you do it like Sills or Pavarotti or croak it like a crow. In or out of tune, it will make sweet music tonight. Let the sounds flow into our ears and the truth stream into our hearts. And do not be afraid to cry. If you are a new creature in Christ you will be happy in your tears.

ALLELUIA is a Hebrew word, and down the centuries the church has brought it with her, untranslated (like "Amen"), as a product of the Jewish soil from which she herself sprang and as a reminder of her earliest days. The word is a cry of jubilation meaning "Praise the Lord," and it occurs frequently in the psalms.

It is wonderful to think that this Easter cry of jubilation has accompanied the church since the days of its childhood; that amid all the ups and downs of almost two thousand years it has been sung over and over again on this night of nights, in the cathedrals and village churches of the entire world, in the certainty that the Lord whom we praise will be with the church until he comes again on the clouds of heaven.

True enough, in the world in which we live there seems reason for everything but the singing of Alleluia. And yet this is the basic hope to which our faith gives us access: that for us as for Christ Good Friday is not a goal but a way station. You may remember that "Pasch," the old name for Easter, has its exact English translation in the name for the Jewish Easter: "Passover." Because we know that our entire life is but a "passing over" to the city of God in which "all her lanes will cry 'Hallelujah'" (Tobit 13:18), therefore even now we can sing "Alleluia — Praise the Lord, for great is his mercy." He intends to lead us, his members, along the victorious way Balthasar Fischer   that he himself has traveled through death to life.

A FTER the sabbath, as the first day of the week was dawning, Mary Magdalene and the other Mary went to see
the tomb. And suddenly there was a great earthquake; for an
angel of the Lord, descending from heaven, came and rolled
back the stone and sat on it. The appearance of the angel
was like lightning, and its clothing white as snow. For fear of
the angel the guards shook and became as if dead. But the
angel said to the women, "Do not be afraid; I know that you
are looking for Jesus who was crucified. He is not here; for
he has been raised, as he said. Come, see the place where
he lay. Then go quickly and tell his disciples, 'He has been
raised from the dead, and indeed he is going ahead of you
to Galilee; there you will see him.' This is my message for
you." So the women left the tomb quickly with fear and great
joy, and ran to tell his disciples. Suddenly Jesus met them
and said, "Greetings!" And they came to him, took hold of
his feet and worshiped him. Then Jesus said to them, "Do
not be afraid; go and tell my brothers to go to Galilee, there
they will see me."

Matthew 28:1 – 10

T HE Lord is risen from the grave:
Alleluia, alleluia!
Who for us hung on the wood:
Alleluia, alleluia!

Monastic liturgy

S ISTER Mary came a-runnin' at the break of day,
Brought the news from heaven, the stone
done roll away!

The soldiers there a-plenty, standin' by the door,
But they could not hinder; the stone done roll away!

Old Pilate and his wise men didn't know what to say,
The miracle was on them! The stone done roll away!

African American
spiritual

YE choirs of new Jerusalem,
your sweetest notes employ,
the paschal victory to hymn
in strains of holy joy.

For Judah's lion bursts its chains,
crushing the serpent's head,
and cries aloud through death's domains
to wake the imprisoned dead.

Devouring depths of hell their prey
at his command restore;
his ransomed hosts pursue their way
where Jesus goes before.

Triumphant in his glory now
to him all power is given;
to him in one communion bow
all saints in earth and heaven.

Fulbert of Chartres
Eleventh century

WHEN the sabbath was over, Mary Magdalene, and Mary the mother of James, and Salome bought spices, so that they might go and anoint him. And very early on the first day of the week, when the sun had risen, they went to the tomb. They had been saying to one another, "Who will roll away the stone for us from the entrance to the tomb?" When they looked up, they saw that the stone, which was very large, had already been rolled back. As they entered the tomb, they saw a young man, dressed in a white robe, sitting on the right side; and they were alarmed. But he said to them, "Do not be alarmed; you are looking for Jesus of Nazareth, who was crucified. He has been raised; he is not here. Look, there is the place they laid him. But go, tell his disciples and Peter that he is going ahead of you to Galilee; there you will see him, just as he told you." So they went out and fled from the tomb, for terror and amazement had seized them; and they said nothing to anyone, for they were afraid.

Mark 16:1 – 8

O miracle! Hades has swallowed Christ the Lord
and has not digested him.
The lion has devoured the lamb, and has not
stomached him.
Death has swallowed life and has vomited in nausea,
even those which it has previously devoured.

A single grain was sown and the whole world is nourished.
As a man he was slaughtered and as God he became alive.
As an oyster he was trampled upon,
then as a pearl he has adorned the church.
As a sheep he was slaughtered
and as a shepherd with his cross for a staff
he has expelled the pack of demons.
As a light on a candelabrum he was extinguished
on the cross, and as the sun he arose from the tomb.

A double wonder could be seen: When Christ was crucified
the day became dark, and when he arose the night became
bright as day.

Asterius of Amasea
Fourth century

Now that we have seen the resurrection of Christ, let us
adore the all-holy Lord Jesus, the only sinless one. We
bow in worship before your cross, O Christ, and we praise
and glorify your resurrection, for you are our God, and we
have no other, and we magnify your name. All you faithful,
come: let us adore the holy resurrection of Christ, for, behold,
through the cross joy has come to the world! Let us always
bless the Lord, let us sing his resurrection, for by enduring for
us the pain of the cross, he has crushed death by his death.

Byzantine liturgy

BUT on the first day of the week, at early dawn, they came to the tomb, taking the spices that they had prepared. They found the stone rolled away from the tomb, but when they went in, they did not find the body. While they were perplexed about this, suddenly two men in dazzling clothes stood beside them. The women were terrified and bowed their faces to the ground, but the men said to them, "Why do you look for the living among the dead? He is not here, but has risen. Remember how he told you, while he was still in Galilee, that the Son of Man must be handed over to sinners and be crucified, and on the third day rise again." Then they remembered his words, and returning from the tomb, they told all this to the eleven and to all the rest. Now it was Mary Magdalene, Joanna, Mary the mother of James, and the other women with them who told this to the apostles. But these words seemed to them an idle tale, and they did not believe them. But Peter got up and ran to the tomb; stooping and looking in, he saw the linen cloths by themselves; then he went home, amazed at what had happened.

Luke 24:1 – 12

I lit my pipe. The smoke of the first puffs built up like sculptures of bluish stone in the shaft of sun; though the month's cold had been relentless, the sun was strengthening every day—at our backs, as it were. "But mightn't our own brains look exactly the same way, to an electrical engineer?"

"In theory, Professor Lambert, but only in theory. In practice, there is something there nobody wants to talk about: you. When you hear a noise—those bulldozers over there, for instance—vibrations compress the air and move through the glass and stone and touch the little bones in your ear, they communicate the disturbance to the eardrum, which passes it on to the fluid of the inner ear, and that moves some filaments that generate electrical impulses that travel along the auditory nerves to the brain. But who is hearing the noise? Not the brain by itself; it's just a mass of electro-chemical jelly. It doesn't hear anything, any more than a radio hears music it plays. Who, furthermore, decides to get up and go to the window and see what's making the noise? Something makes those neurons fire that move the muscles that move your body. That something is nonphysical: a thought, a desire. People are willing to admit that the brain affects the mind — creates the mind, you could say — but, illogically, don't accept the other side of the equation, that mental events create brain events. Yet it happens all the time. The world we live in, the subjective world, is a world of mental events, some of which move our bodies. This is the most obvious fact of our existence and yet materialism asks us to ignore it."

"*Certum est,*" I murmured, "*quia impossibile est.*"

"What's that?" the young man asked. He did not know Latin. But, then, he might say, those who know Latin do not know the language of computers. We all know, relatively, less and less in this world where there is too much to be known, and too little hope of its adding up to anything.

"'It is certain,'" I translated, "'because it is impossible.' Tertullian. His most famous sentence, in fact — usually mis-quoted as *Credo quia absurdum est:* 'I believe because it is absurd.' He never said that. What he was talking about, in the relevant section of *De carne Christi,* is shame, embar-rassment. Intellectual embarrassment. Marcion, the fasti-dious heretic, was evidently embarrassed by God's supposed incarnation in Christ. But what is more unworthy of God, Tertullian asks, more likely to raise a blush — being born or dying? What is in worse taste, being circumcised or cruci-fied? Being laid in a manger or in a tomb? It's all something to be ashamed of. But, 'Whoever is ashamed of me,' God says, 'of him will I be ashamed.' 'I am safe,' Tertullian says, 'if I am not ashamed of my Lord' — nor embarrassed, that is to say, by the incarnation and all the awkwardness that goes with it. The son of God died, Tertullian says: It is absolutely to be believed, because it is out of place, in poor taste — *ineptum,* the Latin adjective is. And was buried, and rose again; it is certain, because it is impossible."

John Updike

I N honor of my resurrection in Christ this day cries out: "In
my journey I beheld a new wonder—an open tomb, a man
risen from the dead, bones exulting, souls rejoicing, men
and women refashioned, the heavens opened and powers
crying out: 'Be lifted up, you everlasting doors, that the king
of glory may come in.'"

Hidden first in a womb of flesh, Christ sanctified human birth
by his own birth; hidden afterward in the womb of the earth,
he gave life to the dead by his resurrection.

Hesychius of Jerusalem
Fifth century

O UR God is good, give thanks!
God's love is for ever!
Our God of gods, give thanks!
God's love is for ever!
Our Lord of lords, give thanks!
God's love is for ever!

Alone the maker of worlds!
God's love is for ever!
Architect for the skies!
God's love is for ever!
Spread land on the sea!
God's love is for ever!

Set the great lights above!
God's love is for ever!
The sun to rule the day!
God's love is for ever!
The moon and stars, the night!
God's love is for ever!

Struck down Egypt's firstborn!
God's love is for ever!
Guided Israel's escape!

God's love is for ever!
Held out a mighty arm!
God's love is for ever!

Split in two the Reed Sea!
God's love is for ever!
Led Israel across!
God's love is for ever!
Drowned Pharaoh and his troops!
God's love is for ever!

Led the desert trek!
God's love is for ever!
Struck down mighty tribes!
God's love is for ever!

Gave Israel a land!
God's love is for ever!
For God's servant to keep!
God's love is for ever!

Remembered our distress!
God's love is for ever!
Kept us from defeat!
God's love is for ever!
God feeds all living things!
God's love is for ever!
God in heaven, be thanked!
God's love is for ever!

Hallelujah!

Psalm 136:1 – 17,
21 – 26

THE text of the Hebrew Exodus has been read and the words of the mystery have been explained: how the sheep was sacrificed for the salvation of the people.

For born Son-like, and led forth lamb-like, and slaughtered sheep-like, and buried human-like, he has risen God-like, being by nature God and human.

He is all things: in as much as he judges, Law; in as much as he teaches, Word; in as much as he saves, Grace; in as much as he begets, Father; in as much as he is begotten, Son; in as much as he suffers, sheep; in as much as he is buried, human; in as much as he has risen, God.

Melito of Sardis
Second century

This is Jesus Christ to whom be glory for ever and ever. Amen.

CRISTES pepull, bothe men and woymen, as ye all knowen wele, thys day ys called in sum plase Astyrday, and in sum plase Pase-day, and in sum plase Godys Sonddy.

Hyt ys called Astyr-day . . . for wel nygh in ych plase hyt ys the maner thys day forto do fyre out of the hall at the Astyr, that hathe all the wyntyr brent wyth fyre and blakyd wyth smoke. Hit shall thys day ben arayde wyth grene rusches, and swete flowres strawed all aboute, scheyng an hegh ensampull to all men and woymen that, rhyght as thay maken clene the howse all wythyn, beryng out the fyre and strawyng flowres, ryyt so ye schull clanse the howse of your soule, doyng away the fyre of lechery and of dedly wrath and of envy, and straw ther swete erbes and flowres; and that ben vertues of goodnes and of mekenes, of kyndnes, of love and charite, of pes and of rest: and soo make the howse of your soule abull to receyve your God. . . .

And rhght as ye clothuth your astyr of your soule, that is, your hert, in fayr clothe of charyte, and of love, and of pes, and of rest wyth all Godys pepull, that ye mow abull be forto recyve the best frende that ye have, that is Crist, Godys sonne of Heven, that thys tyme suffred dethe forto bryng you to the lyfe that ever shall last.

This day is also callyd Pase-day, that is in Englysch, the passyng day. . . . Ych Godys chyld shall passe out of evell

levyng into good lyvyng, out of vyces into vertuys, out of
pride into mekenes, out of covetyse into largenes, out of sloth
into holy bysynes, out of envy into love and charite, out of
wrathe into mercy, out of gloteny into abstynens, out of lechery into chastyte, out of the fendys clochus ynto Godys barm,
and soo of Godys enmy make frende and derlyng. Whosoe
passythe thus, is worty forto come to that gret fest that God
makythe thys day to all that thys passage makut.

Thys day ys called Godys Sonday; for Crist, Godys sonne of
Heven, thys day roos from deth to lyve, and soo gladyth all
hys servantes and frendys. . . . Wherfor all holy chyrch
makythe myrth thys day and syngyth thus: "Thyys ys the day
that our Lord made; be we glad and ioyfull in hure! The
Fadyr of Heven makyth wyth all angelys soo gret melody for
the upryst of the sonne, that makythe thys day a gret passyng
fest, and byddythe all pepull therto, als welehom that ben in
Heven as thylke that ben in erthe.

From an early English
text for preachers
Fourteenth century

L ET all the pious and all lovers of God rejoice in the splendor of this feast; let the wise servants blissfully enter into
the joy of their Lord; let those who have borne the burden of
Lent now receive their pay, and those who have toiled since
the first hour, let them now receive their due reward; let any
who came after the third hour be grateful to join in the feast,
and those who may have come after the sixth, let them not
be afraid of being too late, for the Lord is gracious and he
receives the last even as the first. He gives rest to those who
come on the eleventh hour as well as to those who have
toiled since the first: yes, he has pity on the last and he
serves the first; he rewards the one and is generous to the
other; he repays the deed and praises the effort.

Come you all: Enter into the joy of our Lord. You the first and
you the last, receive alike your reward; you rich and you
poor, dance together; you sober and you weaklings, celebrate the day; you who have kept the fast and you who have
not, rejoice today. The table is richly loaded: Enjoy its royal
banquet. The calf is a fatted one: Let no one go away hungry. All of you enjoy the banquet of faith; all of you receive
the riches of his goodness.

Let none grieve over their poverty, for the universal kingdom has been revealed; let none weep over their sins, for pardon has shone from the grave; let none fear death, for the death of our Savior has set us free: he has destroyed it by enduring it, he has despoiled Hades by going down into its kingdom, he has angered it by allowing it to taste of his flesh.

When Isaiah foresaw all this, he cried out: "O Hades, you have been angered by encountering him in the nether world." Hades is angered because it has been frustrated, it is angered because it has been mocked, it is angered because it has been destroyed, it is angered because it has been reduced to naught, it is angered because it is now captive. It seized a body, and, lo! it discovered God; it seized earth, and behold! it encountered heaven; it seized the visible and was overcome by the invisible.

O death, where is your sting? O Hades, where is your victory? Christ is risen and you are abolished, Christ is risen and the demons are cast down, Christ is risen and the angels rejoice, Christ is risen and life is freed, Christ is risen and the tomb is emptied of the dead: For Christ, being risen from the dead, has become the leader and reviver of those who had fallen asleep. To him be glory and power for ever and ever.

John Chrysostom
Fourth century

H E has risen. A statement like a sea — you cannot walk on it, you cannot build on it, it runs like water through your fingers. He has risen. A statement like a mountain — you cannot see through it, you do not know what lies behind it, you have no idea what it means. Is he here perhaps — a body with eyes that see, with clothes like us?

He is not here. He has risen. This statement appears, without joy or rapture, in tonight's gospel. The first people to hear it ran away in fear and consternation and, in their panic, told nobody anything about it.

This panic need not surprise us. It is no wonder. The fact that we people cannot believe this statement and cannot live it out in our lives, that it is powerless and does not kindle a light in us and that we cannot understand it—this is no wonder. Look at any dead person and you can see nothing of that word "resurrection." And look at so many living people in the world — the dullness, the dreary care, the endless routine, the slavery, the violence, and the apparent desire to keep things exactly the same. The fact that people say that nothing new can ever happen, there is no future, no one can come and deliver me, set me free, the fact that people openly yield to becoming stone, the grave — this despair is no wonder.

But the fact that, even so, in this world, hope still is born, the hope that there will be a hand that rescues and sets us free — someone who does what he says — and that this hope has not yet died, is not yet dead even today, and that this hope still does not die with every dead person — that is the wonder.

No one can say: It will happen to me, as though you know and possess something. No one has ever seen God. But you can say: I hope so. I, for myself, hope I shall be set free. I hope that I shall be allowed to exist, that someone will come for me, that rocks will change into springs and pools, that there will be a city without death.

Huub Oosterhuis

WE must look, yet again, a little deeper into this Christian hope. It is based, not on wishful thinking which longs for continuity when this little life is over. It is the consequence of the belief that God is righteous and that God is love. God made us; God loves us; God will not let us perish.

So the Easter message comes to us once again — comes to us when many hearts are failing for fear, comes to us in an age of uncertainty which for many is the consequence of the abandonment of Christian beliefs. It points us back to the facts apart from which our preaching is vain and your faith is vain — that Christ is risen from the dead, that he has broken the power of death and brought life and immortality to light through the gospel. It points us forward to the day of Christ's ultimate triumph, when he shall reign, and sorrow and sighing shall be no more. It points us to the here and now, to the rough and tumble of discipleship, to the present wrestling with sin and wrong, to the battle for the Lord to which every Christian man and woman is committed.

Donald Coggan

Roman Missal

D EAR friends in Christ,
as our brothers and sisters
approach the waters of rebirth,
let us help them by our prayers
and ask God, our almighty Father,
to support them with his mercy and love.

Tertullian
Third century

T HE Passover provides the day of most solemnity for baptism, for then was accomplished our Lord's passion, and
into it we are baptized.

Aimé Georges
Martimort

T HE whole rite of the holy night is designed to praise both
the Pasch of Christ and baptism or, rather, to celebrate
both the mystery of Christ and Christian initiation as two
aspects of the same reality.

T HE connection between the paschal mystery and baptism seems to be present to the children no less than it
was to Saint Paul. A five-year-old girl had drawn a sheep
following the presentation of the Good Shepherd parable.
Some months later, after the presentation of baptism, she
took out her drawing once again and added a lighted candle
beside the sheep, and explained: "It has the light of Jesus
inside; it's not a sheep like the others, it's in his sheepfold."
Marco, six years old, drew two candles beside a sheep, saying: "It is very happy"; when the catechist asked him why,
Marco replied: "It is with God."

[In her drawing], Carola, six years old, joined together the
sheepfold and the baptismal symbols of the white gown,

light, oils and God's word; the sheep goes to take the light directly from the paschal candle. On the same subject, the drawing of Carlos, six years old, is worthy of note: He has depicted his "becoming a sheep of Jesus" as united to baptism with the eucharist as the point of arrival.

Sofia Cavelletti

THEOLOGIANS have tried to express the power and the richness of baptism, but their efforts are feeble in comparison with the reality of the gift. The liturgy of baptism itself, however, proclaims loudly the effect of that first sacrament: Baptized into the death of Christ and buried with him, we are washed free of sin and live now a new life. Baptism by immersion expresses most succinctly and most dramatically the metamorphosis the sacrament brings about. But the baptismal liturgy is even a veritable sensory feast accosting eye and ear and tongue and nose and skin, insisting that the sacrament touches every part of our beings. Even children can intuit the importance, though not the precise meaning, of such bodily involvement. We make it difficult for our children to appreciate their belonging to the Christian community if, after we baptize them, we do not continue to include them in the initiatory process. Children should be present frequently at the celebration of the sacrament to allow the liturgy both to foster their appreciation of their own privileged membership in the community of faith and to encourage their increasingly responsible participation in community life.

One of the greatest benefits of the revised adult Christian initiation process is its restoration of the role of the community in the reception of new members. And even children can take part in the community action. They can, for example, voice a meaningful and enthusiastic "yes" to a simple questioning as to whether they are willing to live model Christian lives in order to give good example to others soon to join the company of persons, like themselves, who are already consecrated in Christ Jesus as a holy people.

Mary Catherine Berglund

ALMIGHTY and eternal God,
be present in this sacrament of your love.
Send your Spirit of adoption
on those to be born again in baptism.
And may the work of our humble ministry
be brought to perfection by your mighty power.

Roman liturgy

LORD of the passover,
you have lit this night with the radiance of Christ;
renew in us our baptism,
and bring us through the Red Sea waters
to the promised land.

New Zealand
Prayer Book

YOU who love humankind, be gracious,
take pity on those you have created.
Save your creation, the work of your right hand.
With your divine and indescribable beauty,
transform all those who are going to be reborn.

Serapion of Thmuis
Fourth century

IN baptism — because it is an event — the form and the
essence, the "doing" and the "happening," the sign and its
meaning coincide, for the purpose of one is precisely to be
the other, both to reveal and to fulfill it. Baptism is what it
represents because what it represents — death and resurrection — is true. It is the representation not of an "idea" but of
the very content and reality of the Christian faith itself: to
believe in Christ is to "be dead and have one's life hid with
him in God." Such is the central, overwhelming and all-
embracing experience of the early church, an experience so
self-evident, so direct, that at first the church did not even
"explain" it but saw it rather as the source and the condition
of all explanations, all theologies.

Alexander Schmemann

Y OU begin by using symbols, and end by contemplating
them.

Annie Dillard

W HEN the Easter Vigil "speaks" about initiation, it does
so in terms of a veritable evangelization of the cosmos. Fire, wind, wax, bees, light and darkness, water, oil,
nakedness, bread, wine, aromas, tough and graceful words
and gestures: All these stand as a context without which
what happens to one entering corporate faith in Jesus Christ
dead and rising is only partially perceptible.

Aidan Kavanagh

T HE whole initiatic process reinforces this sense that the
fullness of the sacred is invested in the cult objects. Then
in the concluding moments, upon the threshold of a new
life, the illusion is dissolved and the shock of disenchant-
ment shatters all that went before. The experience makes a
return to the previous state of life impossible. The naive real-
ism of the uninitiated perspective has been exploded. The
rites have demonstrated irreversibly that things are not sim-
ply what they appear to be, that one-dimensional literalism
is a childish faith that one has to grow beyond or else despair
of a life rich in meaning and worth. Surely, being thus forced
to abandon one's ingrained notion of reality is to experience
a true death of the former self. And this loss of self constitutes the concrete transformation dignified by the symbolic
dying experienced in the rites. . . .

Acts which seem to spell the end of religion . . . lay bare the
limitations of naive views of reality so that through deep-
ened participation in a religious community and celebration
of the day-to-day events of life in religious ritual, the indi-
vidual may increasingly experience the mysterious fullness
of the sacred, sustaining realm. And a mature sense emerges
that the sacred symbols can reveal the sacred without ever
exhausting its reality.

Sam Gill

S YMBOLS and their meanings must be arrived at through a period of time which is often a long one, requiring much patience, but if you wait out this period of time, if you permit it to clear as naturally as a sky after a storm, it will reward you, finally, with a puzzle which is still puzzling but which, whether you fathom or not, still has the beautifully disturbing sense of truth, as much of that ambiguous quality as we are permitted to know in all our seasons and travels and places of short stay on this risky planet.

Tennessee Williams

A LMIGHTY and everlasting God, who in the paschal mystery established the new covenant of reconciliation: Grant that all who are reborn into the fellowship of Christ's body may show forth in their lives what they profess by their faith.

Book of Common Prayer

African American spiritual

T AKE me to the water, take me to the water, Take me to the water to be baptized!

A procession is formed toward the baptistry, which is detached from the church and is either circular or octagonal, in form. In the center is a large font, with several steps leading down to it. A stream of clear water flows into it from the mouth of a metal stag. Over the font is suspended a canopy, in the center of which is a dove with extended wings.

The procession moves from the church to the baptistry in the following order: The paschal candle (which represents the pillar of fire that guided the Israelites by night to the Red Sea, in whose waters they found salvation) goes first, leading on the catechumens. These follow, having their sponsors on their right hand, for each candidate for baptism is to be presented by a Christian. Then come two acolytes; one carries the holy chrism, the other the oil of catechumens. Next, the clergy; and lastly, the bishop and his assistant ministers. The procession is by torchlight. The stars are brightly shining in the canopy of heaven, and the air resounds with the melodious chanting. They are singing those verses of the psalm, in which David compares his soul's pining after her God to the panting of a stag.

Prosper Guéranger
Nineteenth century

As pants the hart for cooling streams
When heated in the chase,
So longs my soul, O God, for thee,
And thy refreshing grace.

For thee my God, the living God,
My thirsty soul doth pine:
O when shall I behold thy face,
Thou majesty divine?

One trouble calls another on
And gathers overhead,
Falls splashing down, till 'round my soul
A rising sea is spread.

Why restless, why cast down, my soul?
Hope still, and thou shalt sing
The praise of one who is thy God,
Thy health's eternal spring.

Natum Tate
Nicholas Brady
Seventeenth century

See, I am coming soon; my reward is with me, to repay according to everyone's work. I am the Alpha and the Omega, the first and the last, the beginning and the end."

Blessed are those who wash their robes, so that they will have the right to the tree of life and may enter the city by the gates.

"It is I, Jesus, who sent my angel to you with this testimony for the churches. I am the root and the descendant of David, the bright morning star."

The Spirit and the bride say, "Come."

And let everyone who hears say, "Come."

And let everyone who is thirsty come.

Revelation 22:12–14, 16–17   Let anyone who wishes take the water of life as a gift.

THIRSTING ones,
    come to the waters,
says the Lord;
you without money,
Ambrosian liturgy   come and eat, and drink with joy.

WE thirst at first — 'tis nature's act —
    And later, when we die,
A little water supplicate
Of fingers going by.

It intimates the finer want
Whose adequate supply
Emily Dickinson   Is that great water in the west
Nineteenth century   Termed Immortality.

IT is not from the well of Jacob,
nor from the waters made sweet by Moses,
nor from the river of the Jordan
which was sanctified by your baptism
at the hand of John.

But it is from your side, O Christ,
that springs the source of life
through which our debts are forgiven
and our sins cleansed away.

Chaldean liturgy

YOU were led to the holy pool of divine baptism, as
Christ was carried from the cross to the sepulchre.

Cyril of Jerusalem
Fourth century

WE approach the font in the company of the saints who
are described in the Book of Revelation as "a hundred and forty-four thousand . . . out of every tribe of the
children of Israel" and as "a great multitude which no one
could number, from every nation, from all tribes and peoples and tongues," who stand before the throne and the
Lamb in white robes, with palm branches in their hands.

When it is said that they have come out of great affliction
and have washed their robes white in the blood of the Lamb,
this is a metaphorical expression of the truth that all the saints
are the fruit of the paschal mystery.

Adolf Adam

MAY God open to me every pass,
Christ open to me every narrow way,
each soul of holy man and woman in heaven
be preparing for me my pathway.

Irish prayer

Then the litany is sung. In the litany some names of the saints may be added, especially the titular of the church, local patrons and the saints of those to be baptized.

Roman Missal

As suggested by the rubric, the names of other saints have been added in the following list.

Holy Mary, Mother of God   Michael   Gabriel   Uriel

Raphael   Adam   Eve   Abel   Seth   Enoch   Noah

Abraham   Sarah   Hagar   Ishmael   Isaac   Rebekah

Jacob   Leah   Rachel   Judah   Joseph   Benjamin

Tamar   Moses   Miriam   Aaron   Joshua   Rahab

Deborah   Jael   Gideon   Samson   Naomi   Ruth

Hannah   Samuel   Saul   Jonathan   David   Bathsheba

Abigail   Solomon   Nathan   Elijah   Elisha   Hosea

Amos   Isaiah   Micah   Jeremiah   Ezra   Joel

Nehemiah   Susanna   Daniel   Esther   Judith   Joseph

Zechariah   Elizabeth   John the Baptist   Anna

Simeon   Peter and Paul   Andrew   John   James

Mary, Martha and Lazarus   Matthew   Philip and James

Bartholomew   Simon and Jude   Mary Magdalene

Joanna   Salome   Mary Cleophas   Matthias   Junia

Barnabas   Tecla   Timothy   Lydia   Mark   Prisca

Stephen   Clement   Ignatius of Antioch   Polycarp

Perpetua and Felicity   Cecilia   Agatha   Agnes

Barbara   Lucy   Lawrence   Ursula   George

Boniface   Wenceslaus   Stanislaus   Thomas Becket

Thomas More   Isaac Jogues and John de Brébeuf

Charles Lwanga   Maximilian Kolbe   Helen   Basil

Nicholas   Cyril of Jerusalem   Patrick   Brigid   Ambrose

Martin of Tours   John Chrysostom   Jerome and Paula

Monica and Augustine   Leo   Gregory   Anselm

Bernard   John Neumann   Margaret   Isidore

Benedict and Scholastica   Hilda   Francis and Clare

Dominic   Thomas Aquinas   Anthony of Padua

Elizabeth   Louis   Albert   Gertrude   Bridget

Catherine of Siena   Joan   Rita   Angela

Teresa of Jesus   John of the Cross   Rose of Lima

Martin de Porres   Peter Claver   Louise de Marillac

Vincent de Paul   Kateri Tekakwitha   Katharine Drexel

Elizabeth Anne Seton   Thèrése   Frances Xavier Cabrini

Hippolytus
Third century

A T the hour when the cock crows they shall pray over the water.

K ING and Lord of all things,
Creator of the universe,
through the incarnation of your only-begotten Son,
   Jesus Christ,
you have given to all created nature the grace
   of salvation;
you redeemed your creation
through the coming of your unutterable Word.
Look down now from the height of heaven
and cast your eyes on these waters,
fill them with the Holy Spirit.

Let your unutterable Word be in them,
let him transform their power.
Let him give them the power to be fruitful,
let him fill them with your grace,
so that the mystery which is to be accomplished
may bear fruit in those who will be regenerated
and may fill with your divine grace
all those who go down
and are baptized.

Transfigured and regenerated,
Serapion of Thmuis   let them thus be saved
   Fourth century   and judged worthy of your kingdom.

I bless thee, creature of water, through God the Living, through God the Holy, who in the beginning by his word did separate thee from the dry land and did command thee to water the earth in four streams, who in the desert gave a sweetness to thy bitterness, that all might drink thee, and for a thirsty people did bring thee forth from a rock.

I bless thee through Jesus Christ his only son our Lord, who by his power in a wonderful sign at Cana of Galilee did change thee into wine, who walked upon thee with his feet, who was baptized by John in Jordan, who did shed thee from his side, mingled with blood, and commanded his disciples to baptize believers.

Gallican-Celtic liturgy

O celestial flood, be sanctified by the Word of God!
O water that was trodden by the feet of Christ,
    be sanctified.
Thou upon whom the mountains weigh down,
    yet thou are not shut up;
Thou art dashed against the rocks,
    yet thou art not destroyed!
Thou art spread abroad upon the earth and yet dost not fall!
Thou art held up by the firmament on high;
thou dost wash the whole universe about,
    cleansing all things, yet none cleanses thee!

Thou, when the people of the Hebrews took their flight,
    was held back and hardened into ice.
Thou melting upon the high peaks dost bring ruin
    upon the dwellers of the Nile,
and with thy fierce raging dost ever torment the world
    as if it were thine enemy.
Thou art one and the same: the salvation of the faithful,
    the avenger of the wicked.

Moses smote the rock and the rock poured thee forth:
The majesty of God commanded thee to come forth
and thou couldst not hide among the boulders.
Thou art borne upon the clouds and dost make fruitful
    the fields with joyful showers.

Through thee a draught bringing grace and life is poured out
    upon bodies hot with summer heat.

Thou dost move quietly upon thy tiny courses,
>   bringing life and fruitful sap,
lest the dry, lifeless earth deny their proper victuals
>   to our bodies.

The beginning of all things and their end exult in thee,

Old Spanish liturgy   yet God has provided that by thee we might know no end.

G REAT are you, O Lord, and marvelous are your works, and there is no word which suffices to hymn your wonders.

For you, of your own good will, have brought into being all things which before were not, and by your might you uphold creation, and by your providence you order the world. When you joined together the universe out of four elements, you crowned the circle of the year with four seasons.

Before you tremble all the Powers endowed with intelligence. The sun sings to you. The moon glorifies you. The stars meet together before your presence. The light obeys you. The deeps tremble before you. The water-springs are subject to you. You have spread out the heavens as it were a curtain. You have established the earth upon the waters. You have set round about the sea barriers of sand. You have shed abroad the air for breathing.

The angelic Powers serve you. The many-eyed Cherubim and the six-winged Seraphim, as they stand round about and fly, veil their faces in awe before your ineffable glory.

For you, God inexpressible, existing uncreated before the ages, and ineffable, descended upon earth, and took on the semblance of a servant, and were made in the likeness of humanity: For, because of the tender compassion of your mercy, O Master, you could not endure to behold humanity oppressed by the Devil, but you came and saved us. We confess your grace. We proclaim your mercy. We conceal not your gracious acts. You delivered the generation of our mortal nature. By your birth you sanctified a virgin's womb. All creation magnifies you, who have manifested yourself among us. You hallowed the streams of Jordan, sending down upon them from heaven your Holy Spirit, and you crushed the heads of the dragons who lurked there.

Wherefore, O King who loves humanity, come now and sanctify this water by the indwelling of your Holy Spirit. And grant to it the grace of redemption, the blessing of Jordan. Make it the fountain of incorruption, the gift of sanctification, the remission of sins, the remedy of infirmities, the final destruction of demons, unassailable by hostile powers, filled with angelic might. Let those who would ensnare your creature flee far from it. For we have called upon your name, O Lord, and it is wonderful and glorious, and terrible unto adversaries.

Let all adverse powers be crushed beneath the sign of the image of your cross.

But, O Master of all, show this water to be the water of redemption, the water of sanctification, the purification of flesh and spirit, the loosing of bonds, the remission of sins, the illumination of the soul, the laver of regeneration, the renewal of the Spirit, the gift of adoption, the garment of incorruption, the fountain of life. For you have said, O Lord: Wash and be clean. Put away evil things from your souls. You have bestowed upon us from on high a new birth through water and the Spirit.

O Lord, manifest yourself in this water, and grant that those who are baptized here may be transformed; that they may put away from them the old person, which is corrupt through the lusts of the flesh; and that they may be touched with the new person, and renewed after the image of him who created them: that being buried, after the pattern of your death, in baptism, they may in like manner be partakers of your resurrection; and having preserved the gift of your Holy Spirit, and increased the measure of grace committed to them, they may receive the prize of their high calling, and be numbered with the firstborn whose names are written in heaven, in you, our God and Lord, Jesus Christ.   Byzantine liturgy

THE power of the Divinity dwells in the visible waters, and by the force of this power, the waters dissolve the might of the Evil One and of Death. The Evil One and Death are undone by baptism; and the resurrection of the body and the redemption of the soul are preached therein. In the waters, as in a tomb, body and soul are buried, and they die and live again in the pattern of the resurrection that is to be at the end. Baptism fills the office of the grave mystically; and the voice of the baptizer is as the voice of the trump in the latter end.

Narsai
Fifth century

FATHER, you give us grace through sacramental signs, which tell us of the wonders of your unseen power.
In baptism we use your gift of water,
   which you have made a rich symbol
   of the grace you give us in this sacrament.
At the very dawn of creation
   your Spirit breathed on the waters,
   making them the wellspring of all holiness.
The waters of the great flood
   you made a sign of the waters of baptism,
   that make an end of sin
     and a new beginning of goodness.
Through the waters of the Red Sea
   you led Israel out of slavery,
   to be an image of God's holy people,
   set free from sin by baptism.
In the waters of the Jordan
   your Son was baptized by John
   and anointed with the Spirit.
Your Son willed that water and blood
   should flow from his side
   as he hung upon the cross.
After his resurrection he told his disciples:
   "Go out and teach all nations,

baptizing them in the name of the Father,
and of the Son, and of the Holy Spirit."
Father, look now with love upon your Church,
and unseal for it the fountain of baptism.
By the power of the Holy Spirit
give to this water
the grace of your Son, so that in the sacrament of baptism
all those whom you have created in your likeness
may be cleansed from sin
and rise to a new birth of innocence
by water and the Holy Spirit.
We ask you, Father, with your Son
to send the Holy Spirit upon the waters of this font.
May all who are buried with Christ
in the death of baptism
rise also with him to newness of life.

*At the words "We ask you, Father" the paschal candle is lowered
into the waters and held there until the prayer ends.*

*Rite of Christian
Initiation of Adults*

THE presider plunges the lighted paschal candle (the risen Christ) into the baptismal water, the womb of Mother Church, thus fertilizing her that she may become pregnant with the catechumens about to be baptized. In former days, when the celebrant plunged the candle into the water for the third time, he breathed thrice upon the surface of the font in the form of the Greek letter *psi,* asking that the Spirit, *Psyche,* might make the water fruitful for regeneration.

Actually the original method of lighting the paschal fire by striking flint against stone also spoke clearly to medieval sensibility of sexual union, but it has certainly lost that meaning today.

Womanprayer

Ogod, the fountain of life,
to a humanity parched
with thirst,
you offer the living water
of grace,
which springs up from the rock,
our Savior Jesus Christ.

Grant your people the gift
of the Spirit,
that we may learn to profess
our faith with courage
and announce with joy
Italian Sacramentary   the wonders of your love.

We give you thanks, almighty God and Father,
for by the gift of water you nourish and sustain
all living things.
Blessed be God for ever.

We give you thanks that through the waters of the Red Sea,
you led your people out of slavery to freedom
in the promised land.
Blessed be God for ever.

We give you thanks for sending your son Jesus.
For us he was baptized by John in the river Jordan.
For us he was anointed as Christ by your Holy Spirit.
For us he suffered the baptism of his own death
and resurrection,
setting us free from the bondage of sin and death,
and opening to us the joy and freedom of everlasting life.
Blessed be God for ever.

We give you thanks for your Holy Spirit
who teaches us and leads us into all truth,

filling us with his gifts so that we might proclaim the
    gospel to all nations
and serve you as a royal priesthood.
    Blessed be God for ever.

We give you thanks for you have called N. to new life
through the waters of baptism.

Now sanctify this water,
that your servants who are washed in it
may be made one with Christ in his death and resurrection,
to be cleansed and delivered from all sin.
Anoint them with your Holy Spirit
and bring them to new birth in the family of your church,
that they may become inheritors of your glorious kingdom.

We give you praise and honor and worship
through your son Jesus Christ our Lord,
in the unity of the Holy Spirit, now and for ever.
    Blessed are you, our strength and song, and our salvation.

*Book of
Alternative Services*

THE baptismal font has sometimes been referred to as the womb of the church. All Christians are born again, initiated by baptism into the body of Christ, the church. We thus share a baptismal bond of unity with Christ and with the church catholic — all who ever have named, or will name, the name of Jesus and serve Christ as his disciples extending his ministry to all the earth.

This baptismal bond of unity links us with all of our sisters and brothers in Christ. We are joined across the centuries of time, united beyond the bounds of geography and political borders, and gathered into *koinonia* — fellowship, community, communion — of all Christian churches which otherwise seem so fragmented and divided. Baptism bridges our human division and calls us to the essential unity of *one body, one Spirit, one hope, one Lord, one faith, one baptism, one God.*

J. Frank Henderson
Kathleen Quinn
Stephen Larson

WE give you thanks, O gracious God,
for the gifts of water and your Spirit.
In the beginning,
when your Spirit moved over the waters,
you gave order and life to your planet earth.

By the waters of the flood you cleansed the world,
and established with Noah and his family
a new beginning for all people.

In the time of Moses, you led your people
out of slavery through the waters of the sea,
making covenant with them in a new land.

In the fullness of time you sent Jesus Christ,
who was formed in the water of a woman's womb.
In the water of Jordan,
Jesus was baptized and anointed by your Holy Spirit.
In his ministry to the world,
Jesus offered living water to the woman of Samaria,
washed the feet of his disciples,
and sent them forth to baptize all nations
    by water and the Spirit.

And now, with your people of all times and places,
we wait with eager longing
as we look for the city of God,
from which will flow the river of life
for the healing of the nations.
Gracious God,
by the gift of water and your Holy Spirit
you sustain all life.
Thanks be to you, O God.

Almighty God,
by the power of your Holy Spirit
and by the sign of this water,
may those who receive this sacrament
be cleansed from sin through the death of Jesus Christ;

be raised to new life through his resurrection;
and be grafted into his body, the church.

Pour out your Spirit upon them
that they may have power to do your will
and continue forever as servants of Christ
to whom, with you and the Holy Spirit
be all honor and glory
now and forever.

*Book of
Common Worship*

HERE is born in Spirit-soaked fertility
a brood destined for another city,
begotten by God's blowing
and borne upon this torrent
by the church their virgin mother.
Reborn in these depths they reach for heaven's realm,
the born-but-once unknown by felicity.
This spring is life that floods the world,
the wounds of Christ its awesome source.
Sinner, sink beneath this sacred surf
that swallows age and spits up youth.
Sinner, here scour sin away down to innocence,
for they know no enmity who are by
one font, one Spirit, one faith made one.
Sinner, shudder not at sin's kind and number,
for those born here are holy.

*Inscription in the
Lateran baptistry*

CHRIST, Lord and Bridegroom, returns from death to bring
his waiting *ecclesia* light and life. He returns in sacramental presence that we perceive by faith. The absence of
Christ during the first part of the great Pasch comes to an end
with the liturgical celebration of the resurrection in which the
church, too, is reborn and enters into new life. The sacraments of water, spirit and table are the visible signs of his
presence among his people.

Joan Halmo

D o you reject sin so as to live in the freedom of God's children?

Do you reject the glamor of evil and refuse to be mastered by sin?

Rite of Christian
Initiation of Adults   Do you reject Satan, father of sin and prince of darkness?

O LD Satan's just like a snake in the grass —
And a Hallelujah to that Lamb! —
A-watchin' for to bite you as-a you pass —
And a hallelujah to that Lamb!

African American   Chilly water! Chilly water!
spiritual   Hallelujah to that Lamb!

D EAR and true children of the church, I have long desired to instruct you in these spiritual and heavenly mysteries of the church . . . so that you may know the work that has been done in you on this evening of your baptism.

First, you entered the vestibule of the baptistry and, standing there, you listened while facing the west. Then they bade you raise your hand, and you renounced Satan, as if he were actually present . . . Just as the tyrant pursued the people of old as far as the sea, this shameless, impudent demon, the source of all evil, pursues you as far as the fountain of salvation. The tyrant was submerged in the sea; the demon disappears in the waters of salvation.

That is why you were ordered to raise your hand and say to Satan, as if he were actually present: "I renounce you, Satan."

What did you say then, each of you, as you stood there? "I renounce you, Satan, wicked and cruel tyrant!" And you asserted: "Henceforth, I am no longer in your power. For Christ destroyed that power by sharing with me a nature of flesh and blood. He destroyed death by dying; never again shall I be enslaved to you. I renounce you, crafty serpent full of deceit! I renounce you who lurk in ambush, who pretend friendship but have been the cause of every iniquity, who instigated the sin of our first parents! I renounce you, Satan, author and abettor of every evil."

When you renounce Satan, you break off every agreement you have entered into with him, every covenant you have established with hell. Then there opens to you the paradise which God planted in the east and from which disobedience expelled our first parents. It is in order to symbolize this that you turned from the west to the east, the land of light. Then they asked you to declare yourself: "I believe in the Father, in the Son, in the Holy Spirit and in a single baptism of repentance."

Draw strength from the words you spoke and be watchful. For, as we have just read, your adversary, the devil, prowls like a roaring lion, seeking whom he may devour. Formerly death was powerful and could devour. But in the bath of new birth God has dried all the tears from every face. Never again shall you weep; you shall always be on holiday, for you have put on the garment of salvation, Jesus Christ.

Cyril of Jerusalem
Fourth century

To renounce Satan thus is not to reject a mythological being in whose existence one does not even believe. It is to reject an entire worldview made up of pride and self-affirmation, of that pride which has truly taken human life from God and made it into darkness, death and hell. And one can be sure that Satan will not forget this renunciation, this rejection, this challenge: "Breathe and spit upon him!" A war is declared! A fight begins whose real issue is either eternal life or eternal damnation. For this is what Christianity is about! This is what our choice ultimately means!

Alexander Schmemann

THE many references in the writings of the Fathers to the renunciation of Satan demonstrate the great impact that the ceremony made upon the Christian community; and the varied forms in which it appeared show that the formulas and services were constantly adapted in order to make the repudiation of the things of this world, and of the evil genius who ruled over them, more meaningful to the faithful. Nevertheless, the force of tradition is also evident in the retention of the word *pompa* long after the train of the demon gods to which the word referred had ceased to pass in procession through the moldering circuses of the Roman Empire.

Let us glance at the *Acts of St. Sebastian,* a fifth-century literary re-creation of the life and martyrdom of the soldier-saint who died, it was said, during the last persecution of the Christians before toleration came with Constantine the Great. We can see what the renunciation of Satan meant to the author from his account of the conversion of the prefect Chromatius. The theme of renunciation was worked into the prebaptismal course of instruction that the prefect underwent. He was first asked if he renounced all idols. He affirmed that he did. And all sins? He answered that he promised to renounce all the diabolical sins and pleasures of the world. He was told that Lent was the time for candidates to learn that they were to renounce all the arts of the enemy and the commerces of the world. Finally, after a few days, when he had duly renounced all the affairs of the world, he was baptized.

There is nothing of the "pompous" aspect of the devil's empire in this account; it is not the fashionable and dissolute life of the circus that the author marked out for sacrifice to the cause of Christ and salvation but rather the corruption and evils of the workaday world.

Henry Ansgar Kelly

Before baptism takes place, the demons must be rejected. The language of demonology suggests that we contend not against a single supernatural being residing in the earth's core but against innumerable and inexhaustible goads against God. All those interior proddings toward rotten behavior, all the external assaults on health and community, the whisper in my head advising that it's not my problem, the arrogance festering into an international crisis—these are demons all. It does, however, matter immensely that we take evil seriously, that we know it resides both inside and out, that we strive to recognize it, isolate it, and in the power of our baptism destroy it, and destroy it again and again, inside and out, whenever it reappears, as it continually will.

Gail Ramshaw

Do you believe in God, the Father almighty, creator of heaven and earth?

Do you believe in Jesus Christ, his only son, our Lord, who was born of the Virgin Mary, was crucified, died and was buried, rose from the dead and is now seated at the right hand of the Father?

Do you believe in the Holy Spirit, the holy catholic church, the communion of saints, the forgiveness of sins, the resurrection of the body and the life everlasting?

Rite of Christian
Initiation of Adults

Will you continue in the apostles' teaching and fellowship, in the breaking of bread and in the prayers?

Will you persevere in resisting evil, and, whenever you fall into sin, repent and return to the Lord?

Will you proclaim by word and example the Good News of God in Christ?

Will you seek and serve Christ in all persons, loving your neighbor as yourself?

Will you strive for justice and peace among all people and respect the dignity of every human being?

Book of
Common Prayer

The archbishop says to the catechumens:

Barberini Euchologion
Eighth century

Behave with reverence; sign yourselves; remove your clothes and shoes.

But in the original practice of baptism the candidate was plunged into the water naked. Nudity was so common in the Hellenistic-Roman world that this practice was not shocking. Perhaps through this symbolism the candidates for baptism understood what total repentance is better than the modern Christian does. The baptized emerged naked as the newborn babe; and the exhortation that an old life was ended and a new life begun was stoutly supported by the ritual. The candidate symbolically left his entire past behind him. He renounced what he had been to become what he

John L. McKenzie   was not.

Before God no creature is hidden, but all are naked and laid bare to the eyes of the one to whom we must render

Hebrews 4:13   an account.

Baptism's knowledge of Christ is not that of the dining room but of the bath house. It is not a mannered knowledge, for manners, etiquette and artifice fall away with one's clothes. It is a knowledge of appalling candor, hearty and intimate, less intellectual than physical — as when lovers are said to "know" one another. It is more the inspired wisdom of Solomon's Song than of Paul's letter to the Romans. God speaks not only in logic but in the aroma and feel of oil and warm water on the skin, and these too possess their own sort

Aidan Kavanagh   of rigorous logic.

S IN and death they put off and cast away in baptism, after the manner of those garments which our Lord departing left in the tomb.

Narsai
Fifth century

S TRIPPED of your garments you were naked and thus resembled Christ on the cross. There, by his nakedness, Christ despoiled the Principalities and Powers and, by means of the wood, dragged them after him in his triumphal procession.

Now, since the hostile powers were hiding in your members, you could no longer be allowed to wear this shabby tunic. I am speaking, of course, not of the garment people see but of the old self that is being corrupted by the lusts that lead astray. May the soul that has stripped off that garment once and for all not put it on again! Let it say, rather, as the Spouse of Christ says in the Song of Songs: "I have stripped off my tunic, how shall I put it on again?"

What a marvelous thing! You were naked in the sight of all, yet you did not blush. In very truth, you were an image of the first man, Adam, who in the garden was likewise naked and did not blush.

Stripped of your garments, you were anointed from the crown of your head to your feet with the oil of exorcism. Here you became a sharer in the true olive tree and grafted on to the true olive tree, and therefore you share in the anointing that the true olive tree bestows.

Cyril of Jerusalem
Fourth century

Casimir Kucharek

A threefold symbolism appears [in stripping]: putting off the old person and old deeds, imitating Christ who died naked on the cross, and Adam naked in paradise without being ashamed.

WE lead them to a place where there is water and they are reborn in the same way that we were reborn ourselves. They are purified, that is, in the water, in the name of God the Father and Master of the universe, of Jesus Christ, our Savior, and of the Holy Spirit. Christ indeed said: "If you are not born again, you shall not enter into the kingdom of heaven." That it is impossible for those who have once been born to enter again into their mother's womb, is evident to everyone. This is why the prophet Isaiah, whom I mentioned earlier, teaches us the way in which sinners must turn from their sins and repent. He puts it like this:

Wash yourselves, purify yourselves,
remove the evil from your soul,
learn to do good.
Be just to the orphan
and defend the widow.
Then come and let us talk together, says the Lord:
Though your sins were like purple,
they shall become white like wool;
and if they are like scarlet,
they shall become white like snow.
But if you do not obey,
the sword shall devour you.
The mouth of the Lord has spoken this.

Such is the teaching that the apostles have handed down to us on this matter. . . .

On him who wishes to be re-born and repents of his sins, we invoke the name of God, Father and Master of the universe. . . .

Justin Martyr
Second century

This washing is called "enlightenment" because those who are taught in this way are enlightened in spirit.

DESCEND, brothers and sisters marked with the seal, and put on Christ the Lord.
Become yourself part of his noble race.

*West Syrian
baptismal chant
Fifth century*

OWord! the sword of the enemy hath struck me; heal me by thy blood. Speedily tear, with thy spear, the handwriting of my sins, and write my name in the book of life.

Byzantine liturgy

Either or both of the godparents touch the candidate. The celebrant, immersing the candidate's whole body or head three times, baptizes the candidate in the name of the Trinity.

I baptize you in the name of the Father,

He immerses the candidate the first time.

and of the Son,

He immerses the candidate the second time.

and of the Holy Spirit.

He immerses the candidate the third time.

*Rite of Christian
Initiation of Adults*

THRICE has the catechumen entirely disappeared under the water: It has closed over and shrouded him. We have the explanation of this given us by apostle Paul: The water of baptism is the tomb in which we are buried together with Christ, and together with him we rise again to life: the death we suffered was the death of sin; the life we are henceforth to live is the life of grace. Thus is the mystery of Jesus' resurrection repeated, with all its fullness, in those who are baptized.

Prosper Guéranger
Nineteenth century

ONWARD roll the waves, O God,
onward like thunder,
onward like fury.
Thundering above the waters,
high above ocean breakers,
you, God, rise with might.

Psalm 93:3 – 4

BLESSED be God who chose you in Christ.

You are God's work of art, created in Christ Jesus.

You are now God's children, my dearest friends. What you shall be in his glory has not yet been revealed.

Happy are those who have washed their robes clean, washed in the blood of the Lamb!

You have put on Christ. In him you have been baptized. Alleluia, alleluia.

Baptismal
acclamations
Rite of Christian
Initiation of Adults

YOU are made holy, splendid,
newborn like the dawn,
fresh like the dew.

Psalm 110:3

OH, I've been to the sea and I've done been tried,
I been down into the sea!
Oh, I've been to the sea and I've done been tried,
   I been down into the sea!

If you don't believe I've been redeemed,
   I been down into the sea!
Just watch my face for the gospel-gleam,
   I been down into the sea!

I'm born of God, I know I am,
   I been down into the sea!
I'm purchased by the dyin' Lamb,
   I been down into the sea!

Hallelujah, and a hallelujah!
Lord! I've been down into the sea!

African American
spiritual

THE next rite has no counterpart in the *Rite of Christian Initiation of Adults,* or in the accounts of Cyril, Chrysostom, Theodore or Hippolytus: The bishop, assisted by the clergy, washes the neophytes' feet. It was, however, practiced in Turin, in Gaul, in North Africa and possibly in Rome.

St. Ambrose is aware of an attempt to explain the ceremony as an injunction upon the neophyte to perform humble service to others in the spirit of our Lord's words, "If I then, your Lord and Teacher, have washed your feet, you also ought to wash one another's feet." He insists, however, that the ceremony is principally a sacramental rite; its effect is to afford protection against the liability to sin inherited from Adam:

"In baptism all guilt is washed away. The guilt has disappeared; but Adam was tripped and thrown by the devil, so that the devil's poison infected his feet; so you have your feet washed, in order to receive the special help of sanctification in the place where the serpent lay in ambush so that he cannot trip you up again. You have your feet washed to wash away the serpent's poison. It also profits our own humility, in that we are not ashamed to do as a mystery what we might refuse to do as an act of homage which is unworthy of our position."

Edward Yarnold

HAVING finished all the sacramental ceremonies, we also handed over to you the *mandatum* by example and by word: For we washed the feet of each of you, calling you forth to our imitation of our Lord and Savior himself, so that you would also wash the feet of your guests. Thus we would teach you not only to be hospitable but also humbly hospitable, so that you would accept them whom you honor in your hospitality and so that you would not be ashamed to fulfill the office of slaves for them.

If you should think that this is injurious to yourselves, and puffed up by devilish pride should disdain to perform the Lord's *mandatum,* and, although you are of noble stature in this age, you are ashamed to wash the feet of a poor and contemptible Christian in this world, then you are ashamed of Christ.

Anonymous Veronese
preacher
Fifth century

B APTISM is the source of "re-membering." It tells us "who
we are and who we are becoming," as John the Deacon
wrote in the year 500. It tells us that we are the Christ, daily
being made more and more into his image. This is dangerous and subversive information. Those who regard human
life as worth little are able to countenance any sort of social
injustice. Those who know themselves as images of God
have a profound sense of dignity and worth born of knowing
their divine heritage; and, aware that every other person is
also the Christ, they are not satisfied until economic and
social structures provide dignity and care for all.

The early church's baptismal liturgy was an experience of
social justice, of a new social order, the reign of God. By
modeling a new creation, in the catechumenate and in baptism, the early church subverted the Roman Empire from
within rather than challenging it head on. . . . Christians proclaimed in word and deed that only Jesus, who had accomplished their liberation by his death and resurrection, was
the Lord. This undercut allegiance to the Roman imperial
system. It is no wonder the Roman Empire persecuted the
Christian community. . . .

By choosing voluntarily to forego food, the faithful have made
themselves powerless, too. They are ready to stand with the
"marginal" of their own community, those called to baptism
this Easter. They discover that, contrary to our society's wisdom, sharing their goods does not deprive them of worth or
being; rather, it enables them to be filled with the sense of
wholeness and "new creation" that is the heart of the Easter
Vigil. This is what the Fathers called "festive fasting." When
we choose to be dispossessed of material good, we redis-
cover it as sacramental; we learn that it is meant to lead us
to relationships, not to be an end in itself. . . .

Adult baptism at the Easter Vigil shows the world how God
sees the human race. As Nathan Mitchell has noted, the
experience of a catechumen in baptism is radically in con-
trast with the usual experience of interaction in daily life.
Where else does one experience being lovingly bathed, mas-
saged with perfumed oil, clothed in a beautiful new garment,
embraced, fed, incensed? Yet these are true symbols of the
way God sees us; as we act out this love at the Easter Vigil,
we reveal the new humanity that God is working to build.   *Robert Brooks*

*Rite of Christian
Initiation of Adults*

YOU have become a new creation
and have clothed yourselves in Christ.
Receive this baptismal garment
and bring it unstained to the judgment seat
    of our Lord Jesus Christ,
so that you may have everlasting life.

Coptic liturgy

THE baptizer shall clothe the person that has been baptized in a white garment, and shall say: A garment of
eternal and immortal life! Amen.

I sing out with joy to the Lord,
all I am delights in God,
for the Lord has dressed me
in robes of justice and victory,
like a groom wearing a garland
or a bride arrayed in jewels.

The world will see your deliverance,
all kings witness your glory.
They will know you by a new name
which the Lord will give you.
Your walls and towers will shine forth,
a royal crown in God's hand.

They will no longer call you Forsaken,
nor your land Barren.
Beloved will be your name,
and your land will be called Married.
For the Lord delights in you,
and your fields will be fertile.

As a young man marries a wife,
your Builder will marry you.
As a groom delights in his bride,
Isaiah 61:10; 62:2–5   the Lord will honor you.

W HILE you place the robe upon him, you say:
Receive the white robe, and bear it spotless before
the judgment seat of our Lord Jesus Christ. Amen.

Missale Gothicum

T HE postbaptismal vesting in the "robe of light" signifies
above all the return to the integrity and innocence we
had in paradise, the recovery of our true nature obscured and
mutilated by sin. St. Ambrose compares the baptismal robe
to the vestments of Christ on Mount Tabor. The transfigured
Christ reveals perfect and sinless humanity as not "naked"
but vested in garments "white like snow" in the uncreated
light of divine glory. It is paradise, not sin, that reveals our
true nature; it is to paradise and to our true nature, to our
primordial vestment of glory, that we return in baptism.

Being thus the fulfillment of baptism, the rite of the white
garment inaugurates the next act of the liturgy of initiation.
We are vested in this "shining robe" so that we may be
anointed. In the early church there was no need to explain
the organic and self-evident connection between the two
rites. The church knew the three essential connotations of
this double action, revealing the three fundamental dimen-
sions of our "high calling" in Christ—the *royal,* the *priestly,*
and the *prophetic.* The linen ephod of King David, the sac-
erdotal vestments of Aaron and his sons, the mantle of Elijah,
the "setting apart" of the king and the priest through anointment, the prophetic gift as "anointment": all this is fulfilled
in Christ who "has made us kings and priests, a chosen generation, a royal priesthood, a peculiar people," who in the
last days has poured out his spirit so that we "shall prophesy."
Born again in the baptismal font, "renewed after the image
of him who created us," restored to our "ineffable beauty,"
we are now ready to be "set apart" for our new and high
calling in Christ. Baptized into Christ, having put on Christ,
we are ready to receive the Holy Spirit, the very spirit of
Christ, the very gifts of Christ the Anointed—the king, the
priest and the prophet—the triune content of all genuine
Christian life, of all Christian "spirituality."

Alexander Schmemann

SEE those people dressed in white,
God's gonna trouble the water.
They must be the children of the Israelites,
God's gonna trouble the water.

See those people dressed in black,
God's gonna trouble the water.
They come a long way and they ain't turning back,
God's gonna trouble the water.

See those people dressed in blue,
God's gonna trouble the water.
They look like people coming through,
God's gonna trouble the water.

See those people dressed in red,
God's gonna trouble the water.
They must be the children that Moses led,
God's gonna trouble the water.

Wade in the water,
Wade in the water, children,
  wade in the water,
God's gonna trouble the water!

*African American
spiritual*

BESTOW upon me the shining tunic,
you who are clothed with light as with a mantle,
most merciful Christ, our God.

*The Ordo
of Constantinople*

CHILDREN of the baptismal font, all newly baptized,
As you are giving thanks, let us cry out to thee,
    Christ, God,
"Baptize us in the light of thy countenance,
    Clothe us in the robe worthy of thy marriage.
Glory to thee, glory to thee because thou hast consented to
    Our resurrection."

Romanos
Sixth century

THE wedding feast of the Lamb begins.
The bride is radiant, clothed in glory.
Alleluia, Alleluia!

Revelation 19:7

THE place before the great sanctuary in which you will
stand immediately after your baptism symbolizes the
glory of the world to come. The singing of psalms with
which you will be received is a prelude to the hymns of
heaven. The lamps you will light prefigure that great procession of lights in which we shall go to meet the bridegroom with the bright lamps of faith, our souls radiant and
pure. Very careful shall we be not to fall asleep, in case the
awaited one should arrive unexpectedly. Nor shall we come
without the oil of good works, for fear of being excluded
from the bridal chamber.

Gregory of Nazianzus
Fourth century

LET Christ the glor'ous lover
Have everlasting praise;
He comes for to discover
The riches of his grace.
He comes to wretched sinners
To woo himself a bride,
Resolving for to win her
And will not be deny'd.

She bolts the door upon him,
And bids the Lord depart;
She will not serve his honor,
Nor let him have her heart.
Yet Jesus loves the sinner
And will not leave the door,
But cries, beloved creature!
Reject my grace no more.

She now begins to languish,
And none can her relieve;
Her heart is full of anguish
To find she can't believe.
Her hopes are now departed
And left her full of woe.
With all the brokenhearted,
She cries what shall I do?

But Jesus has compassion
Still moving in his breast.
Behold your great salvation!
Come unto me and rest!
One glimpse of love and pow'r
Makes her forget her pain.
She cries, O happy hour!
Is this the lovely Lamb?

Is he whom I rejected
Stoop'd down to me so low?
Goodness, but unexpected,
It hardly can be true;
And still she cries more fervent,
Lord, don't thy mercy hide.
May I become a servant
And fit to be a bride.

The marriage is made ready,
The parties are agreed:

The lily of the valley,
The rose of Sharon's seed.
The bride is now attir'd
With raiment clean and white.
Her sins are freely pardon'd,
And she's her Lord's delight.

They eat and drink together
and mut'ally embrace.
Both saints and angels wonder
At the surprising grace.
This union shall continue
For evermore the same,
And nothing part asunder
The Christian and the Lamb.

The Christian Harmony

M Y sweete spouse, will we go play?
Apples be ripe in my gardene;
I shall clothe thee in new array,
   Thy meat shall be milk, honey and wine.
Now, dear soul, let us go dine,
   Thy sustenance is my scrippe, lo!
Tarry not now, fair spouse mine,
   Quia amore langueo.

Anonymous
Fourteenth century

A s babes from the midst of the womb . . . they are lifted
up from the midst of the water; and as babes everyone
embraces and kisses them. Instead of swaddling clothes they
cast garments on their limbs, and adorn them as a bridegroom on the day of the marriage supper.

Narsai
Fifth century

The celebrant takes the Easter candle in his hands or touches it, saying to the godparents:

G ODPARENTS, please come forward to give to the newly baptized the light of Christ.

A godparent of each of the newly baptized goes to the celebrant, lights a candle from the Easter candle, then presents it to the newly baptized.

Then the celebrant says to the newly baptized:

You have been enlightened by Christ.
Walk always as children of the light
and keep the flame of faith alive in your hearts.
When the Lord comes, may you go out to meet him
with all the saints in the heavenly kingdom.

*Rite of Christian
Initiation of Adults*

T HE Creator Logos, who became incarnate in Christ Jesus, walked in the liturgy as he had walked in the cool of the Garden of Eden and asked the man and the woman who had told them they were naked (Genesis 3:8-13); who stands now amidst a great multitude which no one can number "before the throne and the Lamb, clothed in white robes, with palm branches in their hands, and crying out with a loud voice, 'Salvation belongs to our God who sits upon the throne, and to the Lamb.'" Both scenes, one at the beginning and the other at the consummation of time, are simultaneous in God and exhaustively frame the liturgical assembly at every point in its existence: fallen yet saved by the blood of the Lamb who is Jesus the Christ of God, the fresh-faced boy sitting on the orb of the cosmos and hanging dead on a cross. In the liturgy one is dealing with a *noetos* [a "thinking"] that goes beyond what human mind might devise as light goes beyond darkness. To enter its assembly one must undergo *photismos,* enlightenment; only thus can one stand at the table of life, where all give thanks to God for the divine glory revealed in Christ amidst a gathering from the four winds, an *ecclesia* in the midst of which gestates the passion at the heart of the world.

Aidan Kavanagh

AWAKE, O sleeper, and arise from the dead,
And Christ shall give you light.

Light of the resurrection,
Begotten before the Morning Star
Who gives life through his radiance!

*Ancient baptismal
acclamation*

LET your light so shine before others that they may see
your good works and glorify your Father in heaven.

*Lutheran Book
of Worship*

THE light of faith makes us see what we believe.

Thomas Aquinas
Thirteenth century

*Then having asked the name, let him place a burning candle in the
hand of the infant, saying:*

RECEIVE a lamp burning and without fault: guard thy baptism: Keep the commandments, so that when the Lord comes to the wedding thou mayest meet him together with the saints in the heavenly hall, that thou mayest have eternal life and live for ever and ever. Amen.

Sarum Missal

G OD our maker,
source of all growth in holiness,
accept the joyful thanks and praise
we offer in the name of your church.

In the beginning, at your command,
the earth produced fruit-bearing trees.
From the fruit of the olive tree
you have provided us with oil for holy chrism.
The prophet David sang of the life and joy
that the oil would bring us in the sacraments of your love.

After the avenging flood,
the dove returning to Noah with an olive branch
announced your gift of peace.
This was a sign of a greater gift to come.
Now the waters of baptism wash away sins,
and by the anointing with olive oil
you make us radiant with your joy.

At your command,
Aaron was washed with water,
and your servant Moses, his brother,
anointed him priest.

This too foreshadowed greater things to come.
After your Son, Jesus Christ our Lord,
asked John for baptism in the waters of Jordan,
you sent the Spirit upon him
in the form of a dove
and by the witness of your own voice
you declared him to be your only, well-beloved Son.
In this you clearly fulfilled the prophecy of David,
that Christ would be anointed with the oil of gladness
beyond all others.

And so, Father, we ask you to bless this oil
you have created.
Fill it with the power of your Holy Spirit

through Christ your Son.
It is from him that chrism takes its name
and with chrism you have anointed
for yourself priests and kings,
prophets and martyrs.

Make this chrism a sign of life and salvation
for those who are to be born again in the waters of baptism
Wash away the evil they have inherited from sinful Adam,
and when they are anointed with this holy oil
make them temples of your glory,
radiant with the goodness of life
that has its source in you.

Through this sign of chrism
grant them royal, priestly and prophetic honor, and clothe
    them with incorruption.
Let this be indeed the chrism of salvation
for those who will be born again of water
    and the Holy Spirit.
May they come to share eternal life
in the glory of your kingdom.

Consecration of Chrism
Roman liturgy

WHEAT, the olive and grapes, created for our use —
the three of them serve you symbolically in three
    ways.
With three medicines you healed our disease.
Humankind had become weak and sorrowful
    and was failing.
You strengthened humankind with your blessed bread,
and you consoled it with your sober wine,
and you made it joyful with your holy chrism.

Ephraem of Syria
Fourth century

THE trees once went out
    to anoint a king over themselves.
So they said to the olive tree,
   "Reign over us."
The olive tree answered them,
   "Shall I stop producing my rich oil
   by which gods and mortals are honored,
and go to sway over the trees?"

Judges 9:8 – 9

WE are used to hearing that the oil anoints us all to be kings and queens, to be priests and prophets like the anointed ones of old. But Cyril reverses the image. We are not to reign, either over ourselves or over one another. Rather, we are to be filled with the oil of Jesus Christ the olive tree. Ah, brilliant metaphor, Cyril: for what is the olive tree but the tree that rejected monarchy in order to be pressed out in service for others?

The oil, says Cyril, symbolizes our participation in "the fatness of Christ," a richness that becomes our honor, not imaged as a monarch's crown but as a living tree producing its olives, providing for others that they might have life, life more abundantly. We are so dry, so dried up, that we need the oil from Christ the olive tree to anoint us back to life. Then, as the psalmist sings, we become "like a green olive tree in the house of God."

Many different trees have been used to symbolize God's life. The eighteenth-century poet Joshua Smith called Christ the apple tree, "laden with fruit and always green." At Christmastime, the evergreen stands in our homes as a sign of Christ flourishing in the middle of winter. The dogwood's flower suggests to some people the cross with its traces of blood. The biblical images of the vine, the mustard bush and the cross itself are none of them even self-respecting trees, yet all paradoxically are trees of life. For many poets, preachers and hymnwriters, Christ is the mythic tree of life, bearing its twelve fruits, a tree beyond nature as our life in Christ is beyond our nature.

But at baptism Christ is the olive tree. Our struggles with the flood are finally over, we have been saved in the ark, and the dove flies to us with an olive branch in its beak. It is as Paul wrote to the Romans: The Spirit of God brings us Christ, the peace that passes all understanding. The peace is achieved not by an aggressive monarch, swaying over sub-jugated peoples but by a nurse rubbing oil on an aching body, a Good Samaritan pouring oil on our wounds, a cook preparing the best possible meal with the finest possible oil.   Gail Ramshaw

How glorious you are surrounded by the people:
Like the morning star among the clouds,
like the full moon at the festal season;
like the sun shining on the temple of the Most High,
like the rainbow gleaming in splendid clouds;
like roses in the days of first fruits,
like lilies by a spring of water,
like a green shoot on Lebanon on a summer day;
like fire and incense in the censer, like a vessel
        of hammered gold studded with all kinds
        of precious stones;
like an olive tree laden with fruit, and like a cypress
        towering in the clouds.   Sirach 50:5 – 10

O Lord of mercy and Father of lights,
the giver of every good and perfect gift,
grant to us, unworthy though we be,
the grace to fulfill the ministry of his great
        and lifegiving mystery,
as you gave it to Moses your faithful steward,
        and to Samuel your servant,
and to your holy apostles,
and send your Holy Spirit upon this chrism:

Make it a royal anointing, a spiritual anointing,
a safeguard of life, a hallowing of souls and bodies,
an oil of gladness,
which was prefigured in the Law,
and which shone forth in the new covenant:

For by it were anointed priests and high priests,
prophets and kings, and your holy apostles,
and all who have been reborn through the washing
        of new birth,
by them, and by the bishops and priests who have
        followed them, even to this day.

So, Lord God Almighty, by the coming of your holy
        and adorable Spirit,
make this chrism a garment of immortality, a perfecting seal
which imprints your divine name,
and that of your only-begotten Son, and that
        of your Holy Spirit,
on those who have received your divine washing:

that they may be known before your face,
that they may be of your household and of your city,
        your servants and handmaids;
that they may be delivered from all evil and redeemed
        from all sin;

that they may be recognized by the angels and archangels
and all the powers of heaven

as having put on the garment of your immaculate glory,
and may strike fear into all evil and impure
    demonic powers;

that they may be a people set apart, a royal priesthood,
    a holy nation,
signed through this immaculate mystery,
so that you, O God and Father,
may dwell in them through the Holy Spirit.

For you, our God, are holy,
and you dwell in the holy places among those
    who are holy,
and to you do we give glory,
to the Father, and to the Son, and to the Holy Spirit,
now, and always, and for ever and ever.

Blessing of chrism
Byzantine liturgy

OLIVES are the most civilized of trees. Tending olive trees requires experience and a technical mastery which makes them belong very clearly to the domain of Athene, the goddess of craftsmanship. Olive trees, like agriculture in general, suffer badly in wartime. In Attica, where olive oil was the country's chief export, burned olive groves spelled disaster. So olive branches, evergreen and civilized, came to mean "peace."

The olive tree represented wisdom not only in the sense of technical skill but also because peace is wise and can be preserved only through intelligence and civilized restraint. Olive branches were carried and worn as crowns by suppliants and heralds in the ancient world, much as a white flag signifies surrender and a nonbelligerent attitude today. Suppliants, like sacred olive trees, should be safe from violence, no matter what the politics or what vengeful feelings may be rampant. They constitute a demand for self-control on the part of the powerful.

Winners at the ancient olympic games received a crown of olive leaves for their prize. This honor implied that the victor possessed all of the civilized virtues associated with the olive branch. According to the olympic ideal, any monetary reward would fall far short of the prize of recognition for true worth.

In medieval Europe, following a tradition going back directly to Jewish and classical times, the anointing of a king or queen with olive oil would be completed by placing the crown of destiny upon the sovereign's head.

The olive wreath, and the bay wreath in honor of Apollo, were customarily worn by all the guests at banquets in the ancient world. Eating together is a sign of peace, trust and civilized conviviality. For the Greeks, wearing olive and bay crowns at dinner also signified their acceptance of human limitation and abhorrence of *hybris*. *Hybris* meant insulting contempt for other people's honor arising from an arrogant misunderstanding of one's own worth and duties. Prometheus, the divine benefactor of humanity, had ordained the wearing of the wreath in memory of the day when he had been set free from bondage.

The olive tree, together with its oil, is a symbol of virginity, because its role is to preserve and to be constant, inviolable and unchanging. Olive-pickers, right into the Middle Ages in some places, had to keep chaste while the harvest was on. Olive oil, once pressed, is pure; it is golden and healing and gives light by preserving the flame of the lamp. In one of the parables of Jesus, the wise virgins were able to keep their lamps full of olive oil as they waited for the bridegroom because they prudently took a supply of oil with them to top off their lamps if need be. They were humble (for in Christianity humility and wisdom are aspects of each other) and therefore not misled into forgetting what they were living for: They were able, as a result, to persevere and to be constant.

The foolish virgins got everything wrong, even their role as virgins.

Margaret Visser

THE scarcity and high price of other perfumes has obliged the Latin church to be content with balm alone in the mixture of holy chrism; but in the Eastern church, where the climate is more favorable than ours, three and thirty species of precious perfumes are put into the oil, and it thus becomes an ointment of exquisite fragrance.

Prosper Guéranger
Nineteenth century

Either or both the godparents place the right hand on the shoulder of the candidate. . . .

B E sealed with the gift of the Holy Spirit.

Amen.

Rite of Christian
Initiation of Adults

I anoint thee with the chrism of holiness, the garment of immortality, which our Lord Jesus Christ first received from the Father, that thou mayest bear it entire and spotless before the judgment seat of Christ and live unto all eternity.

Missale Gothicum

Y OU have been pleased to give to your newly illuminated servants new birth by water and the Spirit and have forgiven all their sins, both voluntary and involuntary. . . . Give to them also the seal of the holy, all-powerful and worshipful Spirit, and the communion of the holy Body and the precious Blood of your Christ.

Byzantine liturgy

B UT according as our Lord was anointed by God the Father, being true king and eternal priest, with a celestial and mystic unguent, so now not only pontiffs and kings, but the whole church is consecrated with the unction of chrism, because it is a member of the eternal king and priest. Therefore, because we are a priestly and royal nation, after baptism we anoint that we may be called by the name of Christ [the anointed one].

Isidore of Seville
Seventh century

ALL-POWERFUL God, Father of our Lord Jesus Christ,
by water and the Holy Spirit
you freed your sons and daughters from sin
and gave them new life.

Send your Holy Spirit upon them
to be their helper and guide.

Give them the spirit of wisdom and understanding,
the spirit of right judgment and courage,
the spirit of knowledge and reverence.
Fill them with the spirit of wonder and awe
in your presence.

*Rite of Christian
Initiation of Adults*

STRETCH out your wings, O holy church,
And greet the simple lambs
whom the Holy Spirit has begotten from the waters.

*West Syrian
baptismal chant*
Fifth century

WHEN you were baptized into Christ and clothed yourselves in him, you were transformed into the likeness
of the Son of God. Having destined us to be his children by
adoption, God gave us a likeness to Christ in his glory, and
living as you do in communion with Christ, you yourselves
are rightly called "Christs" or anointed ones. When he said:
"Do not touch my anointed ones," God was speaking of you.

You became "Christs" when you received the sign of the
Holy Spirit. Indeed, everything took place in you by means
of images, because you yourselves are images of Christ.

Christ bathed in the river Jordan, imparting to its waters the
fragrance of his divinity, and when he came up from them
the Holy Spirit descended upon him — like resting upon like.
So you also, after coming up from the sacred waters of baptism, were anointed with chrism, which signifies the Holy
Spirit, by whom Christ was anointed and of whom blessed
Isaiah prophesied in the name of the Lord: "The Spirit of the
Lord is upon me, because he has anointed me. He has sent
me to preach good news to the poor."

The oil of gladness with which Christ was anointed was a spiritual oil; it was in fact the Holy Spirit, who is called the *oil of gladness,* the source of spiritual joy. But you also have been anointed with oil, and by this anointing you have entered into fellowship with Christ and have received a share in his life. Beware of thinking of this chrism as merely ordinary oil. As the eucharistic bread after the invocation of the Holy Spirit is no longer ordinary bread but the body of Christ, so also the oil after the invocation is no longer plain ordinary oil but Christ's gift which by the presence of his divinity becomes the instrument through which you receive the Holy Spirit.

Cyril of Jerusalem
Fourth century

J UDITH took ivy-wreathed wands in her hands and distributed them to the women who were with her; and she and those who were with her crowned themselves with olive wreaths. She went before all the people in the dance.

And Judith sang this song of praise:

Begin a song to my God with tambourines,
    sing to my Lord with cymbals.
I will sing to my God a new song:
O Lord, you are great and glorious,
    wonderful in strength, invincible.
Let all your creatures serve you,
    for you spoke, and they were made.
You sent forth your spirit, and it formed them;
    there is none that can resist your voice.

Judith 15:12 – 13;
16:1, 13 – 14

Y OU shall be a crown of beauty in the hand of the LORD,
    and a royal diadem in the hand of your God.

Isaiah 62:3

T HE one who wrestles has something to hope for; where the contest is, there is the crown. Thou wrestlest in the world, but thou art crowned by Christ, and thou art crowned for contests in the world; for though the reward is in heaven yet the earning of the reward is placed here.

Ambrose
Fourth century

I N peace,
let us pray to the Lord.

For peace from on high,
and for the salvation of our souls.

That the Lord Jesus Christ, our Savior,
may grant us triumph and victory
over the temptations of our visible and invisible enemies.

That we may crush beneath our feet
the prince of darkness and his powers.

That Christ may raise us with him
and make us rise from the tomb,
of our sins and offenses.

That he may fill us with the joy and happiness
of his holy resurrection.

That we may deserve the grace of entering
into the chamber of his divine wedding feast
and rejoice beyond limit,
together with his heavenly attendants
and the hosts of saints glorified through him
in the church triumphant in heaven.

For you are our light and our resurrection,
O Christ our God,
and we send up glory to you
and to your eternal Father
and to your all-holy, good and life-giving Spirit,
now and always and for ever and ever.

Byzantine liturgy

FOR the newly baptized, it is the first time to join the church in its work of interceding. Until now, they have been dismissed before this moment. Perhaps it is difficult for us to understand the meaning of this as we have attached little importance to the work of intercession. Still there is insight for us in the discipline of those periods when the unbaptized never joined in intercession and the baptized saw intercession as both the privilege and the duty that went with baptism. The baptized were to be the voice reminding God of the poor and the church and the troubles of the world. It was practically a job description.

Gabe Huck

IN intercession I turn my neighbor's actual need to God. This means that I see my neighbor, my sister, my brother, my world from the standpoint of what God has promised to and for us. I see my neighbor in the light of God's promise. I also see my neighbor in the light of my neighbor's actual need and yearning. I cannot turn a deaf ear to his or her cry, for in prayer I myself utter that cry *as though it were my own.* So on behalf of the other and in the place of the other I give voice to the other's need for God, both generally and concretely. It is here that for the first time we begin to bear one another's burdens.

Theodore W. Jennings

BLESSED ones, whom the grace of God awaits, when you ascend from that most sacred font of your new birth, and spread your hands for the first time in the house of your mother, together with your brethren, ask from the father, ask from the Lord, that his own specialties of grace and distributions of gifts may be supplied you. "Ask," said he, "and you shall receive." Well, you have asked, and have received; you have knocked, and it has been opened to you.

Tertullian
Third century

THE basic assumption behind the general intercessions is the same as that underlying the liturgy as a whole. It is a keen sense of the relation of this assembly not only to the other churches but also to the world God loves. Even though localized in the place and time of its members, this assembly is a microcosm of Christ's body, a community of baptismal commitment and solidarity, trying to make faith's vision of God's reign serve the rest of the community, the nation and the world. So this assembly has a special relation of representation and advocacy with all those sisters and brothers in the human race whose freedom, dignity and opportunity are curtailed and oppressed by the powers that be, with all who suffer tragedy or misfortune, with all whom the mainstream scorns, demeans, excludes. Our ministry is one of reconciliation.

Robert W. Hovda

Tertullian
Third century

AFTER the prayers, let them give the kiss of peace.

Roman Missal

PEACE be with you.
And also with you.

THERE is a word in Cree — *chiyamayitamowin* — which is used to translate the word "peace." When I was able to understand the root meaning of this word from the elders as I was learning the Cree dialect, I could not help but think how beautiful it was and how theologically appropriate and descriptive. Their word for "peace" is a description of the moment in the spring when, after a rain, all is fresh and green as the sun emerges. It is as though in the calm and beauty of the moment, all of creation is gathering its forces to surge forward to grow, blossom and push toward fruition with the single focus of becoming all it was meant to be. The world is filled with new life and song bringing delight and joy to the Creator and all God's people. That is "peace" from the perspective of the Cree language.

Caleb Lawrence

PEACE!
Peace for us! For everyone!
For all people, this, our hope:
Next year in Jerusalem!
Next year, may all be free!   *A Passover Haggadah*

LET us return to the Lord
who tore us apart
but now will heal us;
who struck us down
yet binds our wounds;
who revives us after two days,
raising us up on the third,
to live in God's presence.   Hosea 6:1 – 2

GREAT and loving Father, your bequest to us in Jesus is
that peace which the world cannot give; your abiding
gift is the Paraclete Spirit he promised.

Quiet our troubled hearts, dispel our anxious fears, that,
confirmed in love and faithful to your word, we may be a
dwelling place fit for you and your Son.   Roman liturgy

PEACE to soothe our bitter woes, God in Christ
        on us bestows;
Jesus bought our peace with God with his holy,
        precious blood;
Peace in him for sinners found is the gospel's joyful sound.

Peace within the church still dwells in her welcomes
        and farewells;
And through God's baptismal pow'r peace surrounds
        our dying hour.   Nikolai Grundtvig
Peace be with you, full and free, now and through eternity.   Nineteenth century

Medieval invitation
to communion

Come, O people, to the holy and immortal mystery, to the necessary offering. With clean hands, let us approach with fear and faith, and share in the gift of our loss, since the Lamb of God was put forth as the sacrifice to the Father. Adore the Lord alone, and give glory with the angels, shouting out: Alleluia!

The Lamb's high banquet we await,
In snow-white robes of royal state:
And now, the Red Sea's channel past,
To Christ our prince we sing at last.

Upon the altar of the cross
His body hath redeem'd our loss:
And tasting of his roseate blood,
Our life is hid with him in God.

That paschal eve God's arm was bar'd,
The devastating angel spar'd:
By strength of hand our hosts went free
From Pharaoh's ruthless tyranny.

Now Christ, our Paschal Lamb, is slain,
The Lamb of God that knows no stain,
The true oblation offer'd here,
Our own unleaven'd bread sincere.

O thou, from whom hell's monarch flies,
O great, O very sacrifice,
Thy captive people are set free,
And endless life restor'd in thee.

For Christ, arising from the dead,
From conquer'd hell victorious sped:
And thrust the tyrant down to chains,
And paradise for us regains.

Early Latin hymn

COME to the feast, you choirs of stars
pointing out the one who rises before the morning star.
Come to the feast, air, which extends over the abysses.
Come to the feast, briny water of the sea,
honored by the sacred traces of the footsteps.
Come to the feast, earth, washed by the divine blood.
Come to the feast, soul of the just, aroused
by the resurrection of a new birth.

This is the Pasch:

Common feast of the world:
Proclamation to the earth
of the Father's will for the universe.
Divine dawning of Christ upon the earth;
invisible feast for angels and archangels,
immortal life of the entire world,
fatal wound of death,
indestructible nourishment of humans,
heavenly soul of the universe,
sacred initiation of heaven and earth,   Anonymous homily
prophet of mysteries old and new.   Second century

THE early Christians saw the path of the sun, sinking
blood-red in the west in the evening and rising bril-
liantly from the dark sea after the long night, as an image of
the path of Christ, the sun, from the passion to death and
resurrection. In the liturgy for Easter eve, that most impres-
sive of all the ancient ceremonials, the focal point of the
three days of Easter and the highlight of the church year, this
transition — Christ's Pasch — is staged as a wonderful mystery of the sun.

With the gray of morning, the night Vigil reaches its conclu-
sion: The Lord invites his community — including its newly
baptized and hence newly born members — to his table,
which is laid with the "bread of eternal life" and the "communion cup of everlasting deliverance" because he has sacrificed himself as a grape on the wine press of suffering and,

as wheat being sown upon earth, has by his death brought forth much fruit. Insofar as the celebration of the eucharist at dawn on Easter morning makes it possible meaningfully to experience the transition from night into day, and the transformation from fasting to feast, it provides an all-embracing reflection of the mystery of the pasch as the passover from imprisonment to freedom, from mourning to joy, from the cross to the resurrection, from death unto life, from anticipation unto fulfillment.

Hansjakob Becker

Cᴏᴍᴇ, then, O lovers of Christ, and in our mouths of clay but with pure hearts let us receive in faith, the Passover that is sacrificed and offered in our midst.

Byzantine liturgy

Oʜ, I'm going to set at the welcome table,
Oh, yes, set at the welcome table,
Oh, yes, set at the welcome table
When my work is done.

Oh, I'm going to feast on milk and honey,
Oh, yes, feast on milk and honey,
Oh, yes, feast on milk and honey
When my work is done.

Oh, I'm going to march with the tallest angel,
Oh, yes, march with the tallest angel,
Oh, yes, march with the tallest angel
When my work is done.

Members, don't get weary,
for the work's 'most done!
Oh, keep your lamp trimmed and a-burnin',
for the work's 'most done!

African American spiritual

ONE is the table that is prepared for rich and poor alike. And though a person may be rich, yet to this table the rich can give nothing. And should another be poor, this one shall have no less honor because of poverty in regard to the things which here belong to all. For this favor is from God, and what wonder that it should be for the rich and the poor alike? For the same is the table that is prepared for the poor person, sitting waiting for an alms, as for the emperor adorned with the diadem and clad in the royal purple, to whom the rule of the world is given. Such are the gifts of God who gives, not according to dignity but according to the will and the mind of each.

To this table therefore let the poor and the emperor come with equal confidence and with equal profit; and here more often the poor will be the richer. And why? Because the emperor is involved in a thousand affairs, and like a ship is tossed hither and thither and brought close to many sins. But the poor have to think solely of the need for food, and such a life is passed in tranquillity and freedom from responsibility, like a ship secure in harbor; and so a poor person approaches much more confidently to the sacred table.

Again, in the feasts of the outside world the poor may be sad and unhappy, the rich festive and rejoicing; and not because of food only but also because of dress. For what happens with regard to food happens also with regard to clothing. For when a needy person sees a rich one clad in fine clothing, the needy one is stricken and fancies himself the unhappiest of all. But here this is taken away, for all alike are clothed with the one saving garment: *For as many of you as have been baptized in Christ, have put on Christ* (Galatians 3: 27).

Leo the Great
Fifth century

As a sparrow homing,
a swallow seeking a nest
to hatch its young,
I am eager for your altars,
Lord of heaven's might,
Psalm 84:4   my king, my God.

THE theology of Easter (exemplified by "nature miracle" stories like that of the loaves and fishes) has illumined our understanding of eucharist by showing that the Christian meal is meant to symbolize the generous, abundant, joyful feasting in the kingdom of God that Jesus embodied at a table that was compassionate, inclusive, egalitarian and open to strangers. The implication is that, for Christians, the practice of open commensality ("doing as Jesus did") *is / becomes / constitutes* the very experience of the Risen One's presence and power.

That is why eucharist brings the sacraments of Christian initiation to their completion. Having been washed, anointed and sealed with the spirit, neophytes are led into the eucharistic assembly, where they exercise their priesthood by participating in the most radical act of the church's mission, the act in which the church literally follows its Savior's lead: Bread-breakers become bread broken; the diners become the world's dinner; the body *at* the table becomes the body
Nathan D. Mitchell   *on* the table — for the life of the world.

IN baptism the eucharist begins, and in the eucharist baptism is sustained. From this premier sacramental union
Aidan Kavanagh   flows all the church's life.

B Y bread you are instructed as to how you ought to cherish unity. Was that bread made of one grain of wheat? Were there not, rather, many grains? However, before they became bread, these grains were separate; they were joined together in water after a certain amount of crushing. For, unless the grain is ground and moistened with water, it cannot arrive at that form which is called bread.

So, too, you were previously ground, as it were, by the humiliation of your fasting and by the sacrament of exorcism. Then came the baptism of water; you were moistened, as it were, so as to arrive at the form of bread. But without fire, bread does not yet exist. What, then, does the fire signify? The chrism. For the sacrament of the Holy Spirit is the oil of our fire. . . . Therefore, the fire, that is, the Holy Spirit, comes after the water, then you become bread, that is, the body of Christ.

Augustine
Fifth century

T HE biblical tradition speaks of God's spirit, that is, God's own living and active presence, lively as the wind, lifegiving as breath, burning as fire, filling the whole world and especially poured out on God's chosen ones.

According to John, the spirit of God in our midst is Jesus "coming back." The spirit is the words of Jesus brought to mind in our presence and enlivened so that they also enliven us. The spirit is the unseen Lord present and giving life. The spirit is this community being loved by God and this community coming to see the unseen risen Lord.

We may say that the unseen Lord is especially seen again in this meal, in this bread and cup set out as his presence among us. Here he who has gone away — in death — comes back in that death held out to us in love. And so this meal is full of the spirit of God. This meal is the wind of God, fire of God, breath of God enlivening us as God's chosen ones.

Come and eat. In the meal is all of Easter and all of Pentecost at once, God coming and loving you, Father and Son present in the meal of the spirit.

Gordon Lathrop

I N baptism we join Jesus in his death, or rather he draws us into his own dying. And we emerge partakers all together of his one new life, his one sanctified humanity: a holy people, a communion of saints.

Spiritual life begins in baptism, for it is nothing less than life in the spirit of Christ. It is nourished at the eucharistic table. There the Spirit moves us to prayer. We give thanks and praise to the Father. We remember everything God did to make us one and holy: everything from the creation of the world to the glorification of Jesus. And we ask God to send the Spirit upon the bread and the cup to make them the body and blood of Christ, so that we who share them together may become one body, one spirit in Christ—an everlasting gift to our God, the definitive manifestation of his sanctifying power.

Through the eucharist of the church, the once for all death and resurrection of Jesus are extended into the ongoing movement of history, sanctifying it and claiming it for God and God's own purpose. Successive moments of time are brought together into the fullness of time, the time of Christ, the time when he bursts the gates of hell and enters upon unending life. Thus the time and space of this world are transformed into the place of God's rule and made to reveal Christ as Lord.

Patrick Regan

E. C. Whitaker

A mixture of milk and honey, and a chalice of water were offered, as well as the bread and wine. The bread was administered first, followed by the water, the milk and honey, and the eucharistic cup, in that order.

B LESS, O Lord, these created elements
of water, honey, and milk;
and grant that your servants may drink from that fount
   of eternal living water,
which is the spirit of truth.
Nourish them with this milk and honey,
even as you promised our fathers Abraham, Isaac
      and Jacob,
that you would lead them into the promised land,
into the land flowing with milk and honey.
Unite your servants with the Holy Spirit, Lord,
even as this honey and this milk are commingled:
through which is shown the union of the heavenly
      substance and the earthly
in our Lord Jesus Christ.

Veronese Sacramentary

Y OU ask why milk and honey are placed in a most sacred
cup and offered with the sacrifice at the pasch. The reason is that it is written: "I shall lead you into a land of promise,
a land flowing with milk and honey." The land of promise,
then, is the land of resurrection to everlasting bliss; it is nothing else than the land of our body, which in the resurrection
of the dead shall attain to the glory of incorruption and
peace. This sacramental then, is offered to the newly baptized so that they may realize that no others but they, who
partake of the body and blood of the Lord, shall receive the
land of promise. As they start upon the journey thither, they
are nourished like little children with milk and honey, so
that they may sing, "How sweet are thy words unto my   John the Deacon
mouth, O Lord, sweeter than honey and the honeycomb."   Sixth century

REJOICE with Jerusalem!
Be glad for her,
all who love her.
Share her great joy,
all who know her sadness.

Now drink your fill
from her comforting breast,
enjoy her plentiful milk.

For this is what the Lord says:
"Look! to her I extend
peace like a river,
the wealth of the nations
like a stream in full flood.
And you will drink!

"I will carry you on my shoulders,
cuddle you on my lap.
I will comfort you
Isaiah 66:10–13   as a mother nurses her child."

THE night of the pasch is the new beginning in the deepest sense, the beginning to which the symbolism of
honey pertains in so essential a manner. Here and now the
new creation is taking place; the golden age of the world is
returning; the doors of paradise are swinging open, and the
promised land lies open before us; honey is trickling from
the opened heavens and from the cross and world-tree of
life. Here and now the newly born of the kingdom of heaven
come forth from the fount and receive the cup of milk and
honey as a sign that they are children of God.

An extremely ancient text — the *Letter of Barnabas* — shows
the continuity between liturgical practice and the folk-custom
according to which milk and honey given to the new born

infant as its first food was the equivalent of the act of *sus-ceptio,* that is to say, the legal reception of the child into the community of the family. The *Letter of Barnabas* uses for this the extremely symbolic word *zoopoieîtai,* "made a living being," "brought to life," which shows that this first food gives the child, in the first instance and strictly speaking, not just the right to life but life itself. This is true for both domains covered by the analogy, for the profane as well as for the liturgical. The early Christians thus saw the postbaptismal drink from the cup of honey as really life-giving; it further gave the *infantes* of the church a claim to be received into the family-fellowship of Christ and the church, and to be raised to the dignity of divine childhood. Tertullian's words are to be understood in this sense, when he writes that honey is the food of life through which Christ makes those who are his own into children of God.

Photina Rech

O my pretty Mother's home,
  Sweeter than the honey in the comb!
Come, love, pretty love,
Come, come, come!
Come, love, pretty love,
I want some!

Patsy Williamson
Nineteenth century

THOU hallowed chosen day! that first
  And best and greatest shinest!
Lady and Queen and feast of feasts,
Of things divine, divinest!
On thee our praises Christ adore,
For ever and for evermore.

Come, let us taste the vine's new fruit
For heavenly joy preparing:
In this propitious day, with Christ
His resurrection sharing:

Whom as true God our hymns adore
For ever and for evermore.

Raise, Sion, raise thine eyes! for lo!
Thy scattered ones have found thee:
From east and west, and north and south,
Thy children gather round thee;
And in thy bosom Christ adore,
For ever and for evermore!

O Father of unbounded might!
O Son and Holy Spirit!
In persons three, in substance one,
Of one co-equal merit;
In thee baptiz'd, we thee adore
For ever and for evermore!

John of Damascus
Eighth century

God of mercy,
pour forth upon us the Spirit of your love,
to make one in mind and heart
those you have nourished by these Easter sacraments.

Roman Missal